MAR   2004

The Executioner Always
Chops Twice

OTHER BOOKS BY THE AUTHOR

Ghosts of the Tower of London, Hendon, 1989
Great Escapes from the Tower of London, Hendon, 1998
Beefeaters of the Tower of London, Hendon, 1985
Tortures of the Tower of London, David & Charles, 1986
The Tower of London As It Was, Hendon, 1988
Lords of the Scaffold, Dobby, 2001
Rack, Rope and Red-Hot Pincers, Dobby, 2001
The Book of Execution, Headline, 1994
Family of Death: Six Generations of Executioners, Hale, 1995
Mysteries of the Tower of London, Hendon, 1998
The Who's Who of British Beheadings, Deutsch, 2000
Crowning Disasters: Mishaps at Coronations, Capall Bann, 2001
Regalia, Robbers and Royal Corpses, Capall Bann, 2002
Grave Disturbances: The Story of the Bodysnatchers, Capall Bann, 2002
William Calcraft, Executioner Extraordinaire!, Dobby 2002

The Executioner Always Chops Twice

Ghastly Blunders on the Scaffold

Geoffrey Abbott

Yeoman Warder (ret'd) HM Tower of London, Member of Her Majesty's
Bodyguard of the Yeomen of the Guard Extraordinary

ST. MARTIN'S PRESS ✹ NEW YORK

THE EXECUTIONER ALWAYS CHOPS TWICE: GHASTLY BLUNDERS ON THE SCAFFOLD. Copyright © 2002 by Geoffrey Abbott. All rights reserved. Printed in the United States of America. No part of this book may be used or reproduced in any manner whatsoever without written permission except in the case of brief quotations embodied in critical articles or reviews. For information, address St. Martin's Press, 175 Fifth Avenue, New York, N.Y. 10010.

www.stmartins.com

Library of Congress Cataloging-in-Publication Data

Abbott, G. (Geoffrey), 1922–
The executioner always chops twice : ghastly blunders on the scaffold / Geoffrey Abbott.—1st U.S. ed.
p. cm.
Originally published: Chichester, West Sussex : Summersdale, c2002.
Includes bibliographical references (p. 240).
ISBN 0-312-32563-0
1. Executions and executioners. I. Title.
HV8551.A24 2004
364.66—dc22   2003066809

First published in Great Britain by Summersdale Publishers Ltd

First U.S. Edition: March 2004

10 9 8 7 6 5 4 3 2 1

*Dedicated to the memory of my friend the late,
great hangman Syd Dernley*

ACKNOWLEDGEMENTS

Grateful thanks are due to all the librarians, curators and custodians of newspaper and similar archives who devoted so much time in helping me delve, dig and discover material for this book. Gratitude is also due to those long-since executed gentlemen and women whose facetious last minute quips leaven these pages; for what is life, or even rapidly approaching death, without humour?

I am also greatly indebted to Dr Harold Hillman, formerly Reader in Physiology and Director of Unity Laboratory of Applied Neurobiology at the University of Surrey.

ABOUT THE AUTHOR

Geoffrey Abbott served in the RAF for 35 years before becoming a Yeoman Warder ('Beefeater') and living in the Tower of London. He now lives in the Lake District and acts as a consultant to international film and television companies and is training to become a helicopter pilot.

CONTENTS

INTRODUCTION

In the days when life was short and disease was rife, when existence for the lower classes was a daily struggle to survive and humane consideration for the wrong-doers, as prescribed by the law, was minimal, death on the scaffold, however violent, was accepted by the populace as the norm and, to many, as a regular source of entertainment. No instruction was given to the executioner regarding exactly how he should perform his task and little or no consideration was given to the possible suffering of the victim, for had not he or she attempted to remove or replace the monarch, change the country's religion or committed some other hideous crime?

So why hone the axe razor-sharp? Why go to all the trouble of training a man to aim it accurately and mercifully? Why allow the victim to die quickly on the rope, or die at all, before disembowelling them with the ripping knife, had they been sentenced to be hanged, drawn and quartered? After all, the victims were there to be punished – and punished they were. Deterrence was the name of the game and as a negative can rarely be proven, the question as to whether it worked or not remains unanswered.

The legal responsibility in England for the execution of criminals, by whatever means, was that of the sheriff, the word derived from 'shire-reeve', he being the chief officer of the Crown of each county or shire. That official however, in order to avoid having to do the distasteful job personally, subcontracted it out to anyone who volunteered, and so the task of beheading, hanging, or of drawing and quartering the condemned person, was undertaken by the hangman, the title describing his more usual occupation.

Those who tightened the noose, swung the axe or wielded

the ripping knife were men of their times, most of them lacking sensitivity or imagination, many of them brutal and callous. Employed when the occasion demanded rather than as civil (!) servants, few if any records were kept of their names, and anonymity was also essential to avoid retribution wreaked by the supporters of those they had executed. Loathed and abused by the public at large, their services, however repugnant to the society of the day, were essential, for without them all those engaged in administering the law of the land, the judges and lawyers, the court officials and the juries, would have been totally redundant.

Admittedly some of them, Thrift, Sanson, Schmidt and the like, tried to dispatch their victims in a humane manner, but the very presence of the almost invariably hostile crowds inhibited their efforts. By instinct anti-government, those who attended executions generally classified the executioner as a symbol of authority and targeted him accordingly, but he was also traditionally greeted with almost affectionate abuse (akin to the present-day treatment of football referees). And just as today's soccer fans would not miss a home game for the world, so in the days of public executions the locals seized every opportunity to attend a local hanging or beheading. Should it be the execution of the perpetrator of a particularly horrific crime, residents of nearby towns would pour in by cart, coach and wagon; in the nineteenth century the rail companies would even lay on special excursions with reductions in fares for group-travelling.

These events provided a great day out for the whole family; they would get there early to get a good seat on the specially erected wooden stands, while the more affluent would book rooms overlooking the scaffold and partake of wine and such repasts as cold chicken or pheasant to sustain them through the performance. Piemen and ale-purveyors plied their wares among the spectators, pickpockets thrived, and the ladies of the night worked days for a change.

Crowds of any sort are peculiarly amorphous bodies capable of committing the sort of acts which its individual members would never dream of carrying out. As an integral part of a mob, those around the scaffold never hesitated to direct disparaging remarks towards the executioner, shouting derogatory comments regarding his skill, appearance, doubtful sobriety and parentage; such epithets were sometimes accompanied by easily obtainable missiles such as rotten fruit and vegetables, even the occasional dead cat. Only when a murderer had killed a child or dismembered a female victim did the hangman find any favour with the crowd, and that but rarely.

So it was hardly surprising that when the executioner, exposed and vulnerable as he was in full view of everyone, became distracted and, at times, apprehensive over his personal safety, things went horribly wrong: nooses slipped, wrong levers were pulled, axes and swords wavered off-aim and guillotine blades jammed.

Even in more recent centuries, when executions took place behind prison walls and the executioners themselves were men of conscience and humanity, the scientific advances at their disposal, being more intricate and technical, brought their own problems with them: electrodes dried out, veins eluded the probing syringe, cyanide delivery mechanisms malfunctioned and trapdoors inexplicably failed to fall. Because no system is totally infallible (and executions are operated by human beings with all their failings) blunders were, and still are, inevitable and unavoidable.

Through it all, however, shone the ability of some of the more undaunted victims to retain an almost unbelievable light-heartedness; delivering a blithe quip or wry comment moments before their lives were brought to an abrupt end. Regardless of their crime, one can only admire their courage and wit under such pressure.

PART ONE:

METHODS OF TORTURE AND EXECUTION

METHODS OF TORTURE

The Boots

Among the tortures mentioned in this book, many chroniclers believe that the 'boots' ranked high among those available to the courts; indeed, some called it 'the most severe and cruell paine in the whole worlde.' Whichever variety of this device was used, the victim, even if not subsequently executed, was invariably crippled for life. In the sixteenth and seventeenth centuries this particular method of persuasion was popular in France and Scotland (where it had the deceptively whimsical-sounding name of 'bootikins'), and so distressing was the sight of a victim undergoing this torture that, as Bishop Burnett wrote in his *History*, 'when any are to be struck in the Boot, it is done in the presence of the Council (of Scotland) and upon that occasion almost all attempt to absent themselves.' Because of the members' reluctance, an order had to be promulgated ordering sufficient numbers of them to stay; without a quorum, the process of questioning could not begin.

One type of the device was a single boot made of iron, large enough to encase both legs up to the knees. Wedges would then be driven downwards a little at a time, betwixt leg and metal, lacerating the flesh and crushing the bone, and incriminating questions asked following each blow with the mallet.

Another version, known as the 'Spanish Boot', consisted of an iron legging tightened by a screw mechanism. Heating the device until red-hot either before being clamped on the legs or while being tightened was an additional incentive to confess.

Another type of high boots were made of soft spongy leather, and were held in front of a blazing fire while scalding water was poured over the fiendish footwear. Alternatively, the victim might have to don stockings made of particularly pliable parchment, which would then be thoroughly soaked with water. Again subjected to the heat of the fire, the material would slowly dry and start to shrink, the subsequent excruciating pain soon extracting a confession.

Boiling Water In Boots

Branding

While not an actual torture or a method of execution, it was nevertheless a penalty administered by the executioner and so was equally liable to go horribly wrong. Branding, from the Teutonic word *brinnan*, to burn, was used in many countries for centuries and was applied by a hot iron which seared letters signifying the felon's particular crime into the fleshy part of the thumb, the forehead, cheeks or shoulders. More appropriately, blasphemers sometimes had their tongues bored through with a red-hot skewer.

Branding With Red-Hot Iron

In England the iron consisted of a long iron bolt with a wooden handle at one end and a raised letter at the other. The letters allowed everyone to know not only that someone was a criminal, but also what particular type of crime had been committed, having 'SS' for Sower of Sedition, 'M' for Malefactor, 'B' Blasphemer, 'F' Fraymaker, 'R' Rogue and so on.

Until the practice was abolished in 1832, French criminals were similarly disfigured, the brand being made even more prominent by the application of an ointment comprised of gunpowder and lard or pomade. In medieval times all felons had the fleur-de-lys brand but later forgers had 'F'; those sentenced to penal servitude, 'TF' (*travaux forcés*); for life imprisonment, 'TPF' (*travaux forcés à perpétuité*) and so on.

15

The Rack

As with other instruments of torture, many different types existed but the basic design of the rack consisted of an open rectangular frame over six feet in length that was raised on four legs about three feet from the floor. The victim was laid on his back on the ground beneath it, his wrists and ankles being tied by ropes to a windlass, or axle, at each end of the frame. These were turned in opposite directions, each manned by two of the rackmaster's assistants; one man, by inserting a pole into one of the sockets in the shaft, would turn the windlass, tightening the ropes a fraction of an inch at a time; the other would insert his pole in similar fashion but keep it still to maintain the pressure on the victim's joints while his companion transferred his pole to the next socket in the windlass. The stretching, the gradual dislocation and the questions would continue until the interrogator had finally been satisfied.

A later version reduced the need for four men to two by incorporating a ratchet mechanism which held the ropes taut all the time, the incessant and terrifying click, click, click of the cogs and the creaking of the slowly tightening ropes being the only sounds in the silence of the torture chamber other than the shuddering gasps of the sufferer.

The 'Ladder Rack' was employed in some continental countries. As its name implies, it consisted of a wide ladder secured to the wall at an angle of forty-five degrees. The victim was placed with their back against it, part way up, the wrists being bound to a rung behind at waist level. A rope, tied around the ankles, was then passed round a pulley or roller at the foot of the ladder which, when rotated, pulled the victim down the ladder, wrenching the arms up behind, causing severe pain and eventually dislocating the shoulder blades. To add to the torment, and further encourage a confession, lighted candles were sometimes applied to the armpits and other parts of the body.

The Ladder Rack

Where it was considered that wider publicity would have a greater deterrent value, felons were racked in the open, usually in the marketplace. For that purpose a different version of the rack was utilised. The victim had to lie face-upwards on the ground; arms bound behind and wrists pulled up and secured to a stake. A long rope, tied about the ankles, was then wound around a vertically mounted windlass, the shaft of which, similar to other models, was pierced with holes so that the executioner's minions could insert poles and so rotate it, thereby imposing continuous and maximum strain on the victim's limbs. This version not only dislocated hip and leg joints but also inflicted extra strain on the shoulder blades and elbows because of the already contorted position of the criminal's arms. And should any additional punishment be deemed necessary, the executioner would deliver measured blows with an iron bar.

Water Torture

The Water Torture

This method of persuasion required the prisoner to be bound to a bench, a cow-horn then being inserted into his or her mouth.

Following a refusal to answer an incriminating question to the satisfaction of the interrogators, a jug of water would be poured into the horn and the question repeated. Any reluctance to swallow would be overcome by the executioner pinching the victim's nose. This procedure would continue, swelling the victim's stomach to grotesque proportions and causing unbearable agony, either until all the required information had been extracted, or until the water, by eventually entering and filling the lungs, brought death by asphyxiation.

METHODS OF EXECUTION

The Heading Axe and Block

Being dispatched by cold steel rather than being hanged was granted as a privilege to those of royal or aristocratic birth, it being considered less ignoble to lose one's life as if slain in battle, rather than being suspended by the hempen rope. Such privilege did not necessarily make death any less painful; on the contrary, for although being hanged brought a slow death by strangulation, the axe was little more than a crude unbalanced chopper. The target, the nape of the neck, was small; the wielder, cynosure of ten thousand or more eyes, nervous and clumsy; and even when delivered accurately it killed not by cutting or slicing, but by brutally crushing its way through flesh and bone, muscle and sinew. It was, after all, a weapon for punishment, not for mercy.

Most English executions by the axe took place in London, the weapon being held ready for use in the Tower of London. The one currently displayed there measures nearly thirty-six inches in length and weighs almost eight pounds. The blade itself is rough and unpolished, the cutting edge ten and a half inches long. Its size and the fact that most of its weight is at the back of the blade means that when brought down rapidly the weapon would tend to twist slightly, throwing it off aim and so failing to strike the centre of the nape of the victim's neck. Unlike hangings, executions by decapitation were comparatively rare events, the executioner thereby being deprived of the necessary practice.

A further factor was that the axe's impact inevitably caused the block to bounce, and if the first stroke was inaccurate and so jolted the victim into a slightly different position, the executioner would need to readjust his point of aim for the next stroke: no mean task while being subjected to a hail of jeers, abuse and assorted missiles from the mob surrounding the scaffold.

The heading axe's vital partner, the block, was a large piece of rectangular wood, its top specifically sculptured for its gruesome purpose. Because it was essential that the victim's throat rested on a hard surface, the top had a hollow scooped out of the edges of each of the widest sides; at one side the hollow was wide, permitting the victim to push their shoulders as far forward as possible, the hollow on the opposite side being narrower to accommodate the chin. This positioned the victim's throat exactly where it was required, resting on the flat area between the two hollows. Blocks were usually about two feet high so that the victim could kneel, although the one provided for the execution of Charles I was a mere ten inches in height, requiring him to lie almost prone and thus induce in him an even greater feeling of total helplessness.

Boiled to Death

This horrific penalty was carried out using a large cauldron filled with water, oil or tallow. Sometimes the victim was immersed, the liquid then being heated, or he or she was plunged into the already boiling contents, usually head first. France favoured the latter method and continued to do so until the punishment was abolished by law in 1791. In England, an Act was passed specifically to execute one Richard Roose in that fashion, he having been found guilty of casting 'a certayne venym or poyson into the yeaste or barme wyth whych porrage or gruell was mayde for the famyly of the Byssopp of Rochester and others.' Seventeen members of the household fell ill, two of them dying, and when news of this un-English type of crime reached the Court, Henry VIII was 'inwardly abhorrying all such abhomynable offences, the sayde poysoning be adjudged high treason.' So he was condemned to be 'boyled to death without havynge any advautage of his clergie.'

An alternative method was to use a large shallow receptacle rather than a cauldron; oil, tallow or pitch being poured in. The victim was then partially immersed in the liquid and then fried to death.

Burned at the Stake

Woman Burned At The Stake

This was the dreaded sentence passed on heretics, sorcerers, witches and women found guilty of treasonable acts. Taken to a public site, usually the marketplace, they were either seated on a stool or made to stand in a tar barrel, secured to a stake by means of a chain attached to a hinged iron ring about their necks and ropes or hoops placed around their bodies. Piles of wood would then be heaped waist-high around them and set alight. As the flames rose and the thick smoke billowed forth, the executioner would either speed their demise by removing the stool so that the ring strangled them, or choked them by pulling the chain. Should the conflagration take too fierce a hold, he would be unable to get near, and it would be some hours before the fire abated, leaving a pile of charred and smouldering ashes.

Some heretics were given the special privilege of having small bags of gunpowder fastened beneath their arms or between their legs, the eventual igniting of which brought death more quickly than by the slow mounting of the flames.

Electric Chair

First used in the late nineteenth century in New York's Auburn State Prison, the electric chair consisted of a high-backed piece of oak furniture fitted with straps that secured the victim's head, chest, arms and legs. Two electrodes, metal plates each sandwiched between a rubber holder and a sponge pad moistened with salt solution, were attached to the felon; one to their shaven head, the other to the base of the spine. After a black hood had been positioned over the face, the switch was operated, sending a current of 700 volts through the body for about 17 seconds. After a brief respite a further charge of 1,030 volts was then delivered, with fatal results, although the body was badly burned.

Later experiments to improve conductivity were tried, some victims having their hands immersed in jars of salt water to which electric wires were connected, but this was discontinued when it was ascertained that three electrodes, to the head and each ankle, were sufficient. Similarly, a leather helmet lined with copper screening and damp sponging, wired to the circuitry, was designed, and the requisite voltage finally determined: two one-minute charges of 2,000 volts, with a ten-second interval would, it was estimated, bring about near-instantaneous death, although on occasion more 'jolts' were needed.

Firing Squad

Depending on the country, firing squads vary in both size and armament, from one man with a pistol or two men with machine guns, to up to twelve men with rifles. The target can be the back of the victim's neck, the head or the heart. Generally, a firing squad is of eight to a dozen men, usually soldiers, standing six yards or so from the victim who is blindfolded and tied to a post with a circular piece of white cloth over the heart as an aiming point. Rifles are collected at random by members of the firing squad, one weapon traditionally being loaded with a blank, reputedly to salve their consciences, enabling them to persuade themselves that they were not responsible for the victim's death. However, with modern weaponry a blank-loaded rifle does not 'kick' as does one with a live round, nor is the cartridge ejected from the weapon.

The signals 'Make ready', 'Aim', 'Fire' are given by the officer in charge by word of command, the hand, a wave of a cane or handkerchief, depending on the circumstances. The sergeant in charge of the squad is armed with a pistol and, should the victim show signs of life after the fusillade of shots, he has the responsibility of administering the *coup de grâce*: a shot to the temple.

In many Eastern countries a pistol bullet in the back of the neck of the kneeling victim is deemed adequate; one bullet at a range of two inches being considered more accurate – and economical – than ten or so bullets fired from twenty feet away.

Gas Chamber

First introduced in the state of Nevada in 1924 after its invention by Major Turner of the US Army Medical Corps who had been analysing the effects on casualties caused by gas warfare in World War I, the gas chamber basically consists of a small airtight room made of steel with two plate-glass observation windows (one for the benefit of the spectators, the other for officials to ensure that the execution is proceeding according to plan) and a chimney to vent the fumes afterwards. It is just large enough to contain one or more chairs bolted to the floor, together with other essential equipment including a container of sulphuric acid.

The victims are secured to the chairs by straps and after the officials have vacated the chamber, the door is closed tightly, hermetically sealing the room. The executioner, stationed in an adjoining room, operates a red-painted lever which, through linkwork, rotates a long rod extending into the gas chamber, thereby allowing it to lower a cloth sachet of sodium cyanide pellets into the acid, the resultant chemical reaction generating hydrogen cyanide, prussic acid (HCN). Exposure to three hundred parts of this toxic cocktail to one million parts of air is fatal, and even if the victim attempts to hold their breath, the longer they attempt to do so, the deeper the eventual breath – and the more rapid the death from asphyxiation.

This method of execution poses various hazards, not only for the victim should the routine itself go wrong, but for those in the immediate vicinity. To ensure that only the victim dies by being gassed and not the officials and spectators as well, it is essential that the chamber is completely air-tight, that the seals around the chimney and operating rod, and in particular those around the door and the two windows, are totally effective. To further reduce the risk of a gas leakage, a pump to reduce the air pressure slightly inside the chamber is sometimes incorporated, so that a faulty seal would result in air being sucked in, rather than allowing the poisonous gas to leak out.

Nor do the risks end when the execution is over. For those having to handle a victim after execution by the rope, electric chair, lethal injection or even broken on the wheel, picking up the component body parts must have been messy in the extreme but was hardly dangerous to the individual involved; but carrying out the same task after a gas chamber execution is fraught with risks. Although powerful pumps extract the gas via the chimney before anyone re-enters the chamber, not only does the gas tend to condense on the walls and floor, but the clothes worn by the victim, even his or her very skin, become impregnated with highly toxic prussic acid. All the surfaces within the room and the corpse itself have to be sprayed with neutralising bleach or ammonia, and the members of the prison staff detailed to remove the body have to wear protective clothing and oxygen masks.

The Guillotine

Introduced in France just in time for the multiple executions resultant from the Revolution, the basic guillotine consisted of two six-inch-thick oak uprights, ten feet high and secured by a cross-piece, mounted on a high wooden base. An inch-deep groove, cut vertically down the inner surfaces of each upright, provided the channels down which the triangular-shaped blade travelled. This blade was six inches in depth and weighed fifteen pounds, with an iron block weighing sixty-five pounds mounted on top in order to maximise the speed of descent.

The blade was held in the raised position by a rope which passed through a ring on its top, each end passing through brass pulleys installed high up on each upright, the two lengths of rope then hanging down the outsides of the uprights and secured there. A block of wood, four inches wide and eight inches deep, scooped out to accommodate the victim's throat, was bolted to the base between the uprights. A transverse groove cut across its top allowed the falling blade to be brought to a shuddering halt after it had passed through the victim's neck. Attached to one side of this block was a hinged iron crescent, the lunette (so-called because it resembled a half-moon), which pressed the neck down, thereby holding the head immobile.

A narrow bench extended from the neck block at right-angles to the uprights, and at its free end a plank was hinged, the bascule, against which the victim was held facing the guillotine while their body and legs were quickly strapped to it. The plank was then rapidly pivoted into a horizontal position and slid forward, thereby placing the victim's neck between the two uprights. The iron crescent was instantly dropped into place and, on the release of the rope, the blade would descend, the severed head falling into the waiting basket. The executioner's assistants then rolled the torso into a full-length wicker basket positioned next to the guillotine, into which the head would also be transferred after having been held high for the crowd's acclaim and abuse, the remains later being taken away for an ignominious burial.

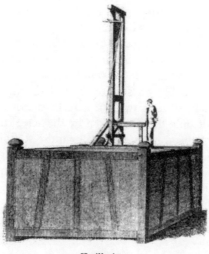

Guillotine

It was acknowledged by those who lived through the French Revolution that the three most unforgettable sounds of those grim days were the 'bang' as the bascule, weighted by the victim's body, fell into the horizontal position; the metallic 'clang' of the lunette falling to pin the neck; and, split seconds later, the 'crash' as the blade, having severed the victim's head, impacted against the lead lining of the groove beneath.

The mechanism was simple and comparatively trouble-free in its action, although it was necessary to ensure that the structure was absolutely level, otherwise the falling blade, being out of true, would jam during its descent; a similar catastrophe was also possible if, due to rain, the two uprights absorbed moisture and became swollen, trapping the blade between them. However, so generally effective was the 'Widow Maker' that, after minor modifications had been incorporated, Monsieur de Paris, the executioner Charles-Henri Sanson (1739–1806) who had dedicated himself to dispatching his aristocratic victims as speedily and therefore as mercifully as possible, perfected his expertise to the extent that eventually he and his highly organised team of assistants were capable of executing 12 victims in 13 minutes, 20 in 42 minutes, 300 in three days and 1,300 in six weeks – a veritable production line of death. This was an incredible achievement when it is realised that these timings included not only the time taken by the actual decapitations, but also by Sanson having to go down the scaffold steps each time, call out the name of the next victim waiting patiently in line, shepherd them up the steps (not easy, their arms being bound behind them) and then manoeuvre them into position facing the bascule.

Hanging

This is possibly the oldest method of execution, doubtless originated by someone who realised that a rope around the neck of a falling body could not slip off because of the projecting mass of the head. Thereafter it was simple to construct a device from which to let the victim fall, and so the gallows came into existence. In twelfth-century England these generally consisted of two uprights joined by a crossbeam capable of accommodating up to ten victims at a time. They would be forced to mount a ladder propped against the beam, the hangman's assistant, straddling the beam, would position the rough hempen rope with its primitive slip knot around their necks, and the hangman would twist the ladder, turning off the victim, death coming slowly and agonisingly by strangulation. As a concession the hangman would sometimes permit the victim's friends or servants to hasten the end by pulling the legs or thumping the chest. The body was then left for an hour before being cut down.

The general practice was to execute the criminal as near as possible to where they had committed the crime, but eventually more permanent sites were established in open areas rather than in the narrow streets and lanes in order to accommodate the vast crowds which would inevitably gather.

London's chief execution site was Tyburn, situated by the main road leading into the capital from the north-west, and it was obvious that the spectacle of the scaffold and the corpses of those who had recently been hanged, swaying on the gibbets, would have the been the greatest deterrent to felons entering the City. Its precise site is difficult to determine, but there is little doubt that the scaffold itself stood near the junction of Edgeware Road and Oxford Street (the latter was once named Tyburn Way) and in fact, should one venture on to the small traffic island there, a plaque will be found, set in the cobbles, bearing the words 'Here stood Tyburn Tree. Removed 1759.'

In 1571, in order to increase production – or rather, extermination – the Tyburn gallows were modified, a third upright and crossbar joining the other two. This triangular arrangement allowed a maximum of twenty-four felons to be hanged at the same time, eight from each arm. The ladder method was also replaced, the victims being brought to the scaffold in a cart which halted beneath the gallows just long enough for the malefactors to be noosed; the horse would then receive a smart slap on the flanks, causing it to move away and take the cart, but not the passengers, with it.

The Triple Tree, About 1680

The last execution took place there on 7 November 1783, after which, due to the expansion of the City's residential suburbs into the Tyburn area, the site was moved to Newgate Prison, executions still being carried out in public outside the walls of that gaol on a portable scaffold which was pulled into place by horses when required. This platform was equipped with two parallel crossbeams positioned over trapdoors: the drop. These were eight feet wide and ten feet long, large enough to accommodate ten felons, and were designed to fall when a short lever was operated. After being noosed and hooded – to conceal their contorted features from the vast crowd of spectators – the victims were allowed to fall a mere three or four feet, thereby dying a slow, lingering death by strangulation, watched by the sheriff and other officials who sat in the comfortable seats arranged at one side of the scaffold.

In England this inhumane 'short drop' method remained unaltered until late in the nineteenth century, when executioner William Marwood introduced the more merciful 'long drop' method in which the distance the victim had to fall depended on his or her age, weight, build and general fitness. The distance was usually between six and ten feet, death coming almost instantly by the dislocation of the neck's vertebrae and severance of the spinal cord. It is often thought that hanging immediately arrests respiration and heartbeat, but this is not so. They both start to slow immediately, but whereas breathing stops in seconds, the heart may beat for up to twenty minutes after the drop.

The last public execution in England took place on 26 May 1868 when Michael Barratt was hanged by executioner William Calcraft for attempting to blow up the Clerkenwell House of Correction in order to rescue colleagues imprisoned therein; the explosion resulted in twelve fatalities and many innocent members of the public were injured. After that date all executions took place behind prison walls, a state of affairs deplored by the public at thus being deprived of what they considered to be their rightful – and free – entertainment, and equally deplored by those who supported the abolition of capital punishment altogether, claiming that being in private, without independent witnesses, executions would become even more brutal.

Hanged, Drawn and Quartered

This was the penalty in England and Scotland for those who, by plotting to overthrow the sovereign by whatever means, were charged with high treason. The method of execution was barbaric in the extreme, as exemplified by the death sentence passed on the regicides who had signed the death warrant of Charles I in 1649. At their trial in 1660 it was ordered:

'that you be led to the place from whence you came, and from there drawn upon a hurdle [a wooden frame] to the place of execution, and then you shall be hanged by the neck and, still being alive, shall be cut down, and your privy parts to be cut off, and your entrails be taken out of your body and, you being living, the same to be burned before your eyes, and your head to be cut off, and your body to be divided into four quarters, and head and shoulders to be disposed of at the pleasure of the King. And may the Lord have mercy on your soul.'

Such appalling punishments were inflicted only on men; women were excused on the grounds of modesty, the reason being, as phrased by the contemporary chronicler Sir William Blackstone, 'for the decency due to the sex forbids the exposure and publicly mangling their bodies.' They were publicly burned instead.

The 'cutting off of the privy parts' was a symbolic act to signify that, following such mutilation, the traitor would be unable to father children who might inherit his treasonable nature; hardly necessary in view of his imminent decapitation.

After the half-strangling, evisceration and dismembering of the victim, the severed body parts were displayed in public as deterrents to others who might attempt such foolhardy acts against the sovereign. The heads, after being boiled in salt water and cumin seed to repel the attentions of scavenging birds, were exhibited in the marketplace or a similar venue in the cities in which the traitors had lived and plotted, the quarters being hung on the gates of those cities. In the capital they were spiked on London Bridge where they remained for months until thrown into the River Thames by the Bridge watchman, usually to make room for new arrivals. As at Tyburn, the grisly exhibits were visible warnings to all entering the City from that direction, of the awful retribution meted out to those who came with criminal intent, or sought to overthrow the realm.

Hanged, Drawn & Quartered

From about 1678 the venue was moved, the heads being displayed within the City itself. Although today Westminster is taken to be just another part of London, it was not always so; originally both were separate cities, one demarcation line between them being an archway named Temple Bar positioned approximately at the juncture of the Strand and Fleet Street. The royal coat of arms was emblazoned above the central arch and the stone heads of the four statues which adorned the edifice, those of Charles I and II, James I and Elizabeth I, were soon joined by the human ones from the Bridge, the prominent position of the archway on such a busy thoroughfare guaranteeing maximum publicity and hopefully deterrence.

Heads On London Bridge

Lethal Injection

More a hospital operation than an execution, the process commences with the condemned person initially receiving an injection of saline solution and a later one of antihistamine; the former to ease the passage of the drugs, the latter to counteract the coughing experienced following the injection of those drugs.

A rapid acting anaesthetic is then administered via a sixteen-gauge needle and catheter inserted into an appropriate vein. The victim next receives pancuronium bromide; this not only has the effect of relaxing the muscles, but also paralyses the respiration and brings about unconsciousness. One minute later, potassium chloride is injected, which stops the heart. This sequence results in the victim becoming unconscious within ten to fifteen seconds, death resulting from respiratory and cardiac arrest within two to four minutes – but only if the correct dosages and intervals between injections are strictly adhered to, otherwise the chemical make-up of the drugs changes adversely.

The risk of such mishaps were ever-present when the drugs were manually administered, but were eliminated to a great extent by a talented technician named Fred Leuchter who invented an automatic, computer-controlled machine which, by controlling an intricate system of syringes and tubing, injects the correct amount of chemicals at precisely the right moment. Fail-safe devices and a manual back-up arrangement are also incorporated into the system and a doctor, stationed behind a screen, constantly monitors the victim's heart condition, thereby being able to confirm the moment of death.

Just as in an execution by firing squad, where a conscience-salving let-out is provided by an unloaded gun, so in an execution by lethal injection, two identical systems are used, neither operator knowing which one is functioning.

Apart from problems brought about by human error or the

malfunctioning of components of the system, difficulties also arise in inserting the syringes into the correct vein, especially where it is narrow or unattainable due to prolonged drug taking by the criminal. It is frequently necessary to make an incision in the flesh and lift out the vein in order to insert the needle.

The Scottish Maiden

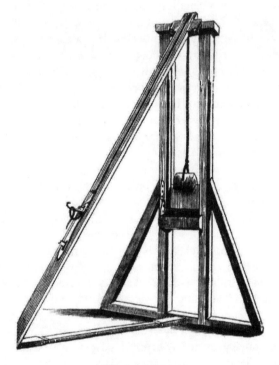

The Scottish Maiden

It is traditionally believed that James Douglas, Earl of Morton, Regent of Scotland, while returning home following a visit to the English court, passed through Halifax, Yorkshire, and in doing so saw the Halifax Gibbet, a guillotine-type machine, although it predated the French device by many decades. Whether an execution was actually taking place at the time is not known, but suffice it to say that so impressed was the Earl that on arriving in Edinburgh he ordered a similar machine to be constructed. It became known as the Scottish Maiden (Madin or Maydin), a name perhaps derived from the Celtic *mod-dun*, the place where justice was administered.

The axe blade, an iron plate faced with steel, thirteen inches in length and ten and a half inches in breadth, its upper side weighted with a seventy-five-pound block of lead, travelled in the copper-lined grooves cut in the inner surfaces of two oak posts and was retained at the top by a peg attached to a long cord which, when pulled by means of a lever, allowed the blade to descend at ever-increasing speed.

Three and a quarter feet from the ground a crossbar joined the two posts, serving as a support for the victim's neck. This beam had a wide groove cut in its upper surface and filled with lead to resist the impact of the falling blade after it had passed through the flesh, muscle and spinal column. To prevent the victim withdrawing their head, an iron bar, hinged to one upright, was lowered and secured to the other upright before the peg was withdrawn and the sentence carried out.

It was operated by the official executioner, the lokman, who was also responsible for its serviceability, it being recorded, for instance, that 'in 1660 Alexander Davidson is to mainteane it all the dayis of his life.' The city accounts reveal that in 1600 the lokman was paid 'twelve shillings and eightpence for one barrell to salt the quarteris with salt thareto', while thirty shillings and fourpence was forthcoming to the lokman 'for the executing and putting up [on display] of the heidis and quarteris.'

Despite its name it showed no favours to females, its blade descending on Isabell and Ann Erskine in 1614 for poisoning their two nephews; Marion Astein for adultery in 1631; and Janet Embrie, found guilty in 1643 of committing incest with two of her brothers.

All executions took place in public, the machine usually being positioned near the City Cross in Edinburgh's High Street, although it could be transported by cart to other cities as required, and many Scottish heads fell beneath its blade between 1564 and 1710, when its use was discontinued.

The Execution Sword

Execution By The Sword (Hans Froschel By Franz Schmidt)

Although rarely used for judicial executions in England, the sword was widely employed on the Continent for dispatching those condemned to death; had it been adopted in England, much unimaginable suffering by the axe's victims could have been avoided, for the execution sword was a finely honed and superbly balanced instrument of death. About three feet or more in length, it weighed approximately four pounds; the blade, two inches wide, had parallel cutting edges and a broad, blunt tip, no point being necessary to achieve its purpose. A 'fuller', a wide groove, ran longitudinally along each side to allow the blood to flow towards the handle and not coagulate and so blunt the razor-sharp edges. The comparatively long handle, designed to be gripped with both hands, was covered with leather or fish skin to provide a non-slip surface. The quillons, the guards, were wide and straight.

Contrary to popular belief, the victim did not kneel over a block. Had they done so, the headsman himself would also have had to kneel and deliver a vertical blow inevitably lacking the force necessary to decapitate his victim. And if, instead of kneeling, he had stood erect, the blade would have struck the further edge of the block rather than the victim's neck. The procedure therefore was for the victim to kneel upright or to stand, the executioner swinging the blade horizontally around his head once or twice to gain the necessary momentum before delivering the fatal stroke. If undue suffering and horrific flesh wounds were to be avoided, 'cooperation' by the victim was essential, for if he or she swayed or trembled too violently, more than one blow would be required.

As the eighteenth-century French executioner Charles-Henri Sanson pointed out,

'It must be taken into account that when there are several condemned persons to be executed at the same time, the terror produced by this method owing to the immense amount of blood that is shed and flows everywhere, creates fear and weakness in the hearts of those who are waiting to die. An attack of faintness forms an invincible obstacle to an execution. If prisoners cannot hold themselves up, and yet the executioner continues with the matter, the execution becomes a struggle and a massacre.'

It was reported that Anne Boleyn, executed by the sword, continued to move her eyes and lips when her severed head was held high. It has been conjectured by some eminent pathologists and neurobiologists that when the head is severed by a sword or a rapidly falling guillotine-type blade, there is sufficient oxygen remaining in the brain to prolong consciousness for perhaps two, three or even more seconds after decapitation.

It is a proven fact that after a person has died, organs surgically removed for life-saving transplant purposes continue to function; hearts to beat, kidneys to produce urine. So if, after being beheaded, the body is not dead, is the severed head still alive? And if the head is still living, is the 'owner' still conscious? If so, could the victim actually see the ground or basket coming up to meet them – even perhaps have sufficient time to witness the gloating faces of those clustered round the scaffold as their head is brandished by the executioner? Alas, like death itself, only those who personally experience decapitation can know what happens and within what timescale.

The Wheel
Being 'broken on the wheel' was an agonising and prolonged way in which to die, and was used mainly on the Continent in

the sixteenth to eighteenth centuries, although isolated cases reportedly took place in Scotland.

The felon was secured, spread-eagled, face upwards, on a large cartwheel mounted horizontally on an upright which passed through the hub, the wheel sometimes being slightly canted in order to give the spectators a better view of the brutal proceedings. The wheel could be rotated in order to bring the particular part of the human target within reach of the executioner, thereby eliminating the need for him to walk round to the other side. Some versions of the device required the victim to be bound to the spokes, others to two lengths of timber in the form of a St Andrew's Cross nailed to the upper side of the wheel.

Breaking On The Wheel Or Cross

41

Death was meted out by the executioner wielding a heavy iron bar, three feet long by two inches square, or using a long-handled hammer. Slowly and methodically he would shatter the victim's limbs; the upper and forearms, the thighs and the lower legs; nor would other parts of the body escape being pulverised, until eventually the *coup de grâce*, known as the retentum, a final blow to the heart or the neck, would be delivered. Alternatively, a cord around the throat would be pulled tight, depriving the victim of what little life was left in them. On being removed from the wheel the corpse would resemble a rag doll, the various short sections of the shattered limbs being completely disconnected from each other.

The judges might mitigate the sentence by permitting the death blow to be administered either following a certain number of strokes or after a certain length of time had elapsed; for example, one John Calas of Toulouse was not to receive a blow to the heart until two hours after he had been strapped to the wheel.

In some states in Germany the regulation number of blows was forty. Franz Schmidt, executioner of Nuremberg in the sixteenth century, wrote in his diary that on 11 February 1585 he 'dispatched Frederick Werner of Nuremberg, alias Heffner Friedla, a murderer who committed three murders and twelve robberies. He was drawn to execution in a tumbrel [a cart], twice nipped with red-hot tongs and afterwards broken on the wheel.'

This multiple murderer was in fact Schmidt's brother-in-law and, probably in view of their relationship, the judges decreed that only thirty-one blows need be struck. One wonders whether, after that number, there was anything worthwhile left to aim at.

PART TWO:

THE UNFORTUNATE VICTIMS

The Axe
Arthur Elphinstone, 6th Baron Balmerino

After the battle against the Scots at Culloden in 1745, Lord Balmerino, Colonel of the Horse Guards, was captured and imprisoned in the Byward Tower of the Tower of London. He was taken to face trial in Westminster Hall, not by being marched through the streets but, unusually, by coach. This departure from tradition caused the authorities some problems, one being where Mr Fowler, the Gentleman Gaoler of the Tower, would travel, for his role was to escort the prisoner at all times. His Lordship solved the dilemma by inviting the officer to accompany him in the coach, not realising that the Gaoler would be carrying the cumbersome Ceremonial Axe, the traditional symbol by which the sentence of the court would be indicated to the crowds waiting outside the Hall; if borne with the edge pointing towards the prisoner, he had been found guilty, and rare it was that it was held facing in the opposite direction.

Carrying the sixteenth-century weapon, its wooden shaft over five feet long, its blade twenty inches wide and ten inches long, the Gaoler climbed awkwardly into the coach, tripping over Balmerino's feet as he did so, whereupon the nobleman shouted, 'Look out – take care, or you'll bark my shins with that damned axe of yours!'

He was evidently fascinated by the weapon however, for as reported by Horace Walpole, 'at the bar, during his trial, he plays his fingers upon the axe while he talks to the Gaoler, and when someone came up to listen, he took the blade and held it like a fan between their faces.'

In his *Official Diary*, Lieutenant-General Adam Williamson,

43

Deputy Lieutenant of the Tower of London, 1722–1747, described the proceedings:

> 'The two Earles [Lords Balmerino and Kilmarnock] had pleaded Guilty the first day and being now call'd to shew cause if they could why Sentence of death should not pass upon them, they spoke their Several Speeches in Mittigation of their crime and to move the Lords to recommend them to the Kings mercie. By the King's command, however, they were ordered to be beheaded.'

The scaffold on Tower Hill was entered via a house on the site which was draped in black for the funereal occasion,

> 'all at the expense of the Sherrifs, and on 18 August 1746 they [the sheriffs] came at ten o'clock precisely and knockt at the Outer Gate of the Tower and demanded the prisoners. We immediately set out from their apartments and I had the doors Lockt after them and the Keys given to Me, that if any Valuable thing was left in them I might secure it as my Perquisite.'

Then followed details of his arrangements for the actual executions:

> 'By the Lords' [the prisoners'] direction the block was desired to be two feet high, and I ordered a good Stiff upright post to be put just under it [to reduce the bounce caused by the impact of the axe]; also a piece of red baize to be had, in which to catch their heads and not to let them fall into the Sawdust and filth of the scaffold, which was done.'

The first execution was that of Lord Kilmarnock,

> 'who had his head sever'd from the Body at one Stroke, all but a little skin which with a little chop was soon separated. He

[Kilmarnock] had ordered one of his Warders to attend him as his Vallet de Chambre and to keep down the body from struggling or violent Convulsive Motion, but it only flounced backward on the Separation of the head and lay on its back with very little Motion.'

Meanwhile Balmerino had been escorted to a small room in the house adjoining the scaffold, where he sipped some wine and nibbled a piece of bread. He was dressed in his regimental uniform, the blue coat with red facings he had worn in the Pretender's Army, and beneath the uniform he wore a woollen shirt which, he said, would serve as his shroud. When the officer in charge delivered the usual speech and concluded with the customary 'God save King George!' Lord Balmerino immediately contradicted the salutation by exclaiming 'God bless King James!', the man he had fought unsuccessfully to place on a Scottish throne.

Another chronicler described how, on being escorted out of the house, 'he saluted the company gathered there and hastened to the scaffold, which he ascended with so undaunted a step as to surprise every spectator.' Once there, he walked around it, bowed to the crowd and read the inscription on his coffin which had been placed at one side in readiness. Then, taking out his spectacles, he read out a paper in which he declared his unshakeable adherence to the House of Stuart, sheer force of habit then causing him to breathe on and wipe them before putting them away in their case. Only then did he turn to the executioner who, dressed in white and wearing a white apron, was waiting nearby. The executioner was John Thrift, a man with a highly nervous disposition; indeed so nervous that he had had to be given a glass of wine before his victim appeared.

As custom demanded, Thrift started to ask Lord Balmerino for forgiveness, but was interrupted, his victim saying that there was no need. However, another custom required that the executioner be paid. Balmerino apologised and, giving him three guineas, said, 'Friend, I never had much money. This is all I have – I wish it were more for your sake. I am sorry I can add nothing else but my coat and waistcoat.'

Taking the garments off, he laid them on the coffin and, calling for the yeoman warder who had been his guardian and companion while he had been imprisoned in the Tower, he gave the man his periwig, replacing it with a nightcap of Scotch plaid, then took the axe from Thrift and, after feeling the edge, returned it to the executioner before finally approaching the block. There, he knelt down, but got to his feet again almost immediately to go round the other side and assume the kneeling position again, where he uttered his last prayer: 'O Lord, reward my friends, forgive my enemies, bless and restore the King, preserve the Prince and the Duke of York [meaning the princes of the House of Stuart] and receive my soul.' Victims were expected to signal their readiness for execution and Balmerino was no exception; throwing up one arm as if charging the enemy in battle, he braced himself for the blow.

Lord Balmerino Beheaded On Tower Hill

What happened next was recorded by General Williamson:

'Lord Balmerino's Fate was otherwais than Kilmarnock's, for tho'
he was a resolute Jacobite and seemed to have more than ordinary
Courage and indifference for death, yet when he layd his head
on the block and made his own Signal for decollation
[decapitation] he withdrew his body a little.'

By this time Thrift was almost in a state of collapse. The object of
all eyes, he somehow managed to raise the axe, trembling as he
did so; feebly he brought it down, Balmerino only sustaining a
flesh wound. The General then reported that 'the bystanders were
forc'd to hold his body and head to the block while the Separation
was making.' At the shout of horror from a thousand or more
throats, again Thrift raised the crude weapon, but again the Scot's
head remained attached to his body. Filled now with panic borne
of desperation, the executioner raised the axe aloft once more, to
bring it down more accurately – the block, indeed the scaffold
itself shuddered with the force of the blow – and Lord Balmerino's
head finally fell onto the piece of red baize which had been spread
out in readiness on the sawdust-strewn boards.

*Ironically enough, after his trial at Westminster, Balmerino, 'keeping his
spirits up, showed Lord Kilmarnock, who had also been found guilty of
committing high treason, how he must lay his head on the block; bade
him not to wince lest the stroke should cut his skull or his shoulders, and
advised him to bite his lips. He also begged that they might have another
bottle together soon, as they should never meet any more till . . .' and
pointed significantly to his neck.*

*Some time later the date and details of Lord Balmerino's execution
were read out to him by the Lieutenant of the Tower while he was dining
in his room. There with him was his wife, she having been permitted to
take her meals with him during his last few days on earth, and on hearing*

the dread news she was not unnaturally overwhelmed with shock and horror. At that, Balmerino exclaimed angrily to the Lieutenant, 'See, sir, with your damned warrant you have spoiled my Lady's dinner!'

Robert Devereux, Earl of Essex

Good-looking, arrogant and self-assured, the Earl of Essex had been extremely popular at one time, winning deserved renown on many battlefields in France and Spain. Becoming Queen Elizabeth's favourite and promoted to Master of the Horse and General of Cavalry, in 1599 she appointed him Governor of Ireland and ordered him to quell the rebels in that country. However, some months later, during a dispute concerning the appointment of a deputy, so insolent was his attitude towards the Queen that she boxed his ears, whereupon he laid his hand on his sword and exclaimed that it was an insult he would not have tolerated from her father (Henry VIII), much less than from a king in petticoats!

His difficulties in Ireland became insurmountable, much to the delight of his rivals at Court, and despite Elizabeth warning, 'We do charge you, as you tender our pleasure, that you adventure not to come out of that Kingdom,' he returned without her permission, appearing in her presence unannounced wearing muddy boots and an unbuttoned doublet. Elizabeth suspended him from most of his offices and, resentful at his downfall from her favour, he conspired against her, even referring to her as 'an old woman, crooked in mind and body.'

On 8 February 1601 he led a body of three hundred fully armed men in a vain attempt to seize the Tower and the Palace of Westminster, but failed abysmally. Taken prisoner, he was charged with having plotted to surprise the Queen at her palace and take her life, to have broken out into rebellion, to have shut up the Lords of the Council, and assaulted the Queen's subjects on the streets.

He confessed everything, even admitting that the Queen could never be safe as long as he lived. The court found him guilty of High Treason and sentenced him to death. Elizabeth, despite her feelings towards him, realised the danger he posed and reluctantly issued the final order for his execution.

On 25 February 1601, the 34-year-old Earl, wearing 'a gown of wrought velvet, a black sattin suit, a felt hat blacke, with a little ruff about his neck,' was escorted by sixteen yeoman warders from his prison in the Develin Tower (now known, appropriately enough, as the Devereux Tower) on to Tower Green. Such was his popularity with the Londoners that the authorities decided to perform the execution within the walls rather than risk a riot by the protesting public if it was carried out, as custom demanded, on Tower Hill.

The executioner was one Derrick, whose life, coincidentally, the Earl had saved when he had been sentenced to death for a rape in Calais, and whose name was later given to a type of crane which resembled a gibbet. Essex asked the executioner whether the waistcoat he was wearing would hinder him or not, and after praying he 'laid himself flat' and put his head in the fatal notch (it appears that the block was very low, requiring the victim to lie prone along the scaffold boards). He then spread his arms out as a signal for Derrick to strike, saying 'Lord, into thine arms I commend my spirit', but the executioner suddenly noticed that the target area, the back of the Earl's neck, was concealed by the collar of his doublet, so told his victim that he must stand up again and remove the garment. 'What I must do, I will do!' exclaimed Essex, and getting up again, took off the doublet and resumed his position along the boards. Once more he spread his arms wide and, as recorded in the ancient annals, 'at three strokes the executioner stroke off his head, and when his head was off and in his executioner's hand, his eyes did open and shut as in the time of his prayer; his bodie never stirred, never any parte of him more than a stone, the first stroke howbeit deadly and depriving him of all sense and motion.'

According to a well-established story, Elizabeth had impatiently awaited the return of a ring which she had once bestowed on him with the assurance that if he were ever in danger and sent it to her, she would interpret it as a plea for pardon which she would assuredly grant. In the Tower, Essex, it seems, intended to take advantage of this royal concession for he gave the ring to the Countess of Nottingham with instructions to pass it to the Queen, but the vengeful Countess deliberately failed to do so. It was not until she lay dying that she confessed to Elizabeth what she had done – alas, too late for Essex.

Consort of Henry VIII, Queen Katherine Howard was found guilty of treason because of her allegedly adulterous life, and sentenced to death. She was committed to the Tower and when, on 12 February 1542, she was informed that she was to be executed by the axe the next day 'she asked that the block might be brought to her room and, this having been done and the executioner fetched, to the amazement of her attendants she knelt and laid her head in the horrible hollow, declaring, as she rose to her feet, that she "could now go through the ordeal with grace and propriety."'

Mary Stuart, Queen of Scots

Executioner Simon Bull was definitely not looking forward to his next assignment, the execution of Queen Elizabeth's cousin, Mary, Queen of Scots who was accused of plotting to assassinate Elizabeth. Hanging was his usual line of work, but this was to be with the axe, with which he hadn't had a great deal of practice.

The execution was ordered to take place on 8 February 1587

in Fotheringhay Castle, Northamptonshire, one of the few times such an event had taken place indoors, but this was considered necessary by the Queen's Commissioners, the Earls of Kent and Shrewsbury, in order to avoid any public unrest should it have occurred in the open. Initially those two gentlemen objected to the doomed Queen being attended by her servants, the Earl of Kent saying that 'they would seek to wipe their napkins in some of your blood [as holy relics], which were not convenient.' Only when she had given her word that they would not do so, was she allowed to choose three or four attendants to accompany her.

A contemporary historian described what happened next.

'After this, escorted by the lords, knights, and gentlemen, the Sheriff leading, she passed into the great hall and stepped up on to the scaffold, this being two feet high and twelve feet broad, with rails about, hanged and covered with black. She sat down on a low stool and, being thus seated, the warrant for her execution was read out. She listened unto it with as small regard as if it had not concerned her at all, and with as cheerful a countenance as if it had been a pardon from her majesty for her life. That done, the Protestant Dean of Peterborough stood in front of her and pressed his administrations, but she rejected them. But the Dean began to pray aloud, whereat she took her beads and a crucifix and said divers Latin prayers.

Her prayers ended, the executioner, kneeling, desired her to forgive him her death; she answered, 'I forgive you with all my heart, for now I hope you will make an end to all my troubles.' Then, with her two women helping her up, began to disrobe her of her apparel. All the time they were so doing, she had never changed her countenance, but with smiling cheer, uttered these words 'that she never had such grooms to make her unready, and that she had never put off her clothes in such a company!' Then being stripped of all her apparel saving her petticoat and kirtle, her two women beholding her made great lamentation and, crying and crossing themselves, prayed in Latin. Turning to them and embracing them, she said, '*Ne crie pas; j'ai promis pour vous.*' Then she bade them farewell, whereupon one of them, having a Corpus Christi cloth, lapped up three corner ways, kissed it and put it over the Queen of Scots' face and pinned it fast to the caul of her head. Then she, kneeling down on the cushion resolutely and praying, groped for the block. Laying down her head and putting her chin over the block, she stretched out her arms and cried out '*In manus tuas Dominie*' three or four times.'

With his assistant holding her still with one hand on her back, Simon Bull brought down the axe, only to have his blow go badly off-aim, striking the knot of the blindfold and apparently stunning her. Again he struck, this time with more success, though in order to sever the head completely, he had perforce to cut through a little gristle with his knife.

The contemporary account continued,

'The executioner then lifted up the head to the view of all the assembly and bade 'God save the Queen' [Queen Elizabeth, of course]. Then, her dressing of lawn [the Corpus Christi cloth] falling off, her head appeared as grey as one of three-score-and-ten years old, cropped very short, her face in an instant being so much altered from the form she had when she was alive, as few could remember her from her face. Her lips stirred up and down a quarter of an hour after her head was cut off. Then one of the executioners espied her little dog which had crept under her clothes, and it could not be gotten forth except by force, yet afterwards would not depart from the dead corpse, but came and lay down between her head and her shoulders, which being imbrued with her blood, it was carried away and washed. All things else that had any blood were either burned or clean washed.'

As evidence that the execution had actually taken place, the late Queen's head was carefully washed and placed on a velvet cushion, then displayed at one of the windows overlooking the vast courtyard for the benefit of the crowds assembled there.

Simon Bull and his assistant were paid their due fees but were not permitted to claim their traditional perquisites of the victim's clothes, thereby depriving them of the opportunity to sell them as holy relics or souvenirs.

John Fisher, Bishop of Rochester, was charged with aiding and abetting treason against Henry VIII and condemned to death. The Pope, Paul III, in defiance of Henry's decision to divorce Katherine of Aragon in order to marry Anne Boleyn, promoted Fisher to cardinal and dispatched a cardinal's hat to the prelate. On hearing of this, Henry VIII, with savage humour, exclaimed, "Fore God, then, he shall wear it on his shoulders!"

M. Rasmussen

Execution by the axe was the method of capital punishment adopted in Denmark until 1887, when Rasmussen, the leader of a gang of highwaymen, was finally caught and sentenced to death. However, when he was escorted on to the scaffold it was discovered that the executioner, doubtless to steady his nerves for the occasion, had imbibed rather too much strong liquor, with disastrous results. Not only did the first blow go badly awry, the next one did also, and it was not until the drunken axeman had swung the weapon for the third time that the head became completely detached from the torso. So outraged were the Danish citizens at this appalling incompetence that following a judicial enquiry, King Christian IX decreed that all capital punishment, both in private and in public, should be abolished forthwith.

George Selwyn, friend of Horace Walpole, regularly attended public executions and on being reproached for being a spectator at the beheading of Lord Lovat in 1747, riposted, 'Well, I made up for it by going to the undertaker's afterwards and watching it being sewn back on again!'

William, Lord Russell

The Rye House Plot of 1683 was a conspiracy to assassinate Charles II and his brother James, Duke of York, near Rye House Farm, Hertfordshire, as they returned from the Newmarket races, a plot in which Lord Russell was falsely accused of being involved. The nobleman was more or less doomed from the start, for his trial was conducted by the Attorney General Judge George Jeffries, who later became known as the infamous Hanging Judge of the Bloody Assizes.

In court Lord Russell asked for a postponement in order to await the arrival of a vital witness. 'Postponement!' exclaimed Jeffries. 'You would not have given the King an hour's notice in which to save his life! The trial must proceed.' Thus prejudged and found guilty, the remainder of the trial was a mere formality, and Lord Russell, found guilty of committing High Treason, was sentenced to be hanged, drawn and quartered, though this was later commuted to just decapitation.

Great efforts were made to save him; his father, the Duke of Bedford, offered the King the phenomenal sum of £100,000 for a royal reprieve, and Lady Russell, the condemned man's wife, went to the court and, throwing herself at Charles' feet, begged him for mercy, but to no avail.

On 21 July 1683 the noble lord was escorted to the scaffold

erected at Lincoln's Inn Fields in London, where awaited the other equally terrifying member of the judicial duo, executioner Jack Ketch. The condemned man surveyed the large, jeering crowd surrounding the scaffold and wryly observed, 'I hope I shall soon see a much better assembly!'

After praying, he removed his peruke (wig), cravat and coat, then handed Ketch ten gold guineas, saying that the executioner should strike without waiting for a sign.

Execution By The Axe

He knelt over the block and Ketch brought the axe down, but only succeeded in inflicting a deep and penetrating wound. Determined to dispatch his victim without further delay, the executioner raised the axe high above his head and brought it down with all the force he could muster; so hard that the blade, passing through most of the victim's neck, embedded itself in the block to such a depth that Ketch, unable to withdraw it, had to sever the head completely by using his knife before holding it high and, in accordance with tradition, shouting, 'Here is the head of a traitor! So die all traitors! God save the King!'

Jack Ketch subsequently blamed the peer for the fact that more than one stroke of the axe was necessary 'because Lord Russell did not dispose himself for receiving the fatal stroke in such a position as was most suitable' and that 'he moved his body while he [Ketch] received some interruption as he was taking aim.'

James Scott, Duke of Monmouth

The illegitimate son of King Charles II by Lucy Walters, the Duke of Monmouth raised an army and sought to overthrow King James II, but was defeated at the Battle of Sedgemoor in 1685. Captured and arrested on 13 July of that year, he was later granted an interview with the King, at which 'he threw himselfe at the King's feete and begged his mercie. It is sayd he was soe disingenious in his answers to what the King askt of him that the Kinge turned from him and bid him prepare for death.'

After the interview King James wrote, 'The Duke of Monmouth seemed more concerned and desirous to live and did not behave himself so well as I expected, nor do as one ought to have expected from one who had taken upon himself to be King. I have signed the warrant for his execution tomorrow.'

On 15 July 1685 he was escorted from the Tower by guards

and also by three officers, each with loaded pistols, for the Duke was extremely popular with the many members of the public who had little time for King James; so popular indeed, that on arriving on the Tower Hill scaffold he was greeted by a chorus of groans and sighs from the gathered throng of spectators. He looked at Jack Ketch, the executioner so notorious for his savage inaccuracy that his name became synonymous with the very word 'hangman'. 'Is this the man to do the business?' he demanded, and when assured that it was, he prayed, then went over to where the block was positioned with the axe resting against it. Picking it up, he felt the edge of it with his nail, then replaced it and, taking six guineas from his pocket and handing them to Ketch, he said, 'Pray, do your business well; do not serve me as you did my Lord Russell, for I have heard you struck him three or four times. If you strike me twice, I cannot promise you not to stir.' Turning to his servant standing next to him, he continued, 'If he does his work well, give him the other six guineas.'

Observers reported that:

'he then proceeded to make himself ready. He took his coat off and laid it down, but his peruke he merely tossed aside. Another short prayer, and then with every appearance of calm he laid himself down before the block and fitted his neck into the notches with much precision. But no sooner had he thus settled himself and the executioner begun to raise the axe, than he raised himself on his elbow and said to the headsman, 'Prithee, let me feel the axe.' Again he ran his finger along the edge. 'I fear it is not sharp enough,' he exclaimed, but the headsman did not like this aspersion on his skill. 'It is sharp enough, and heavy enough,' he assured the doubting Duke. And he had the final word.

Monmouth fitted his head into the block and shut his eyes to await the end.'

Another report had this description:

'the executioner first struck an agitated blow, inflicting a small cut, and Monmouth staggered to his feet and looked at him in silent reproach. Then he resumed his place and the executioner struck again and again. Still the head remained on the block, while his whole body writhed in agony. As the horrified fury of the crowd increased, the headsman threw down the axe, crying, 'I cannot do it. My heart fails me.' 'Take up the axe, man!' roared the Sheriff, while the crowd cried 'Fling him [Ketch] over the rails!' So he took it up and hacked away, but the job had to be finished with a knife. A strong guard protected him as he went off, else he would have been torn to pieces.'

Before being buried in the Chapel Royal of St Peter ad Vincula within the Tower of London, the head was sewn back on to the body for a portrait to be painted by Sir Godrey Kneller, and it is now displayed in London's National Portrait Gallery.

In the Tower of London, awaiting decapitation by the axe for treason against Henry VIII, John Fisher, Bishop of Rochester, discovered that his cook had failed to produce dinner that day. On being questioned, the man explained, 'It was common talk in the town that you should die and so I thought it needless to prepare anything for you.'

'Well,' retorted John Fisher, 'for all that, thou seest me still alive; so whatever news thou shalt hear of me, make ready my dinner, and if thou seest me dead when thou comest, eat it thyself!'

Boiled in Oil
Loys Secretan

In 1488 the tables were neatly turned in the French city of Tours, when the victim, who should have died, didn't, and the executioner, who shouldn't have died, did! Death by immersion in boiling oil was the method of capital punishment in those days, and it so happened that a convicted coiner named Loys Secretan was due to be executed in that manner in the Place de la Fere-le-Roy. Everything went drastically wrong, at least for Denis, the executioner.

'He took the said Loys on to the scaffold and bound his body and legs with cords, made him say his '*in manus*', pushed him along and threw him head first into the cauldron to be boiled. As soon as Secretan was thrown in, the cords became so loose that he twice rose to the surface, crying for mercy. Which seeing, the provost and some of the inhabitants began to attack the executioner, saying, 'Ah, you wretch, you are making this poor sinner suffer and bringing great dishonour on the town of Tours!'

The executioner, seeing the anger of the people, tried two or three times to sink the malefactor with a great iron hook, and forthwith several people, believing that the cords had been broken by a divine miracle, became excited and cried out loudly, and seeing that the false coiner was suffering no harm, they approached the executioner as he lay with his face on the ground, and gave him so many blows that he died.

Charles VIII pardoned the inhabitants who were accused of killing the executioner, and as for the coiner of false money, he was taken to the church of the Jacobins for sanctuary, where he hid himself so completely that he never dared to show his face again.'

Found guilty of committing high treason against James I, George Brooke was condemned to be executed by the axe in the courtyard of Winchester Castle. When he was ordered to lay his head on the block, he told them that 'they must give him instructions what to do, for he was never beheaded before!'

Branding
Comtesse Jeanne de la Motte

One of the most famous cases in which a criminal was disgraced by being disfigured with a brand occurred in France in 1786, the criminal being no less than a lady of society, Jeanne de Saint-Valois, wife of the Comte de la Motte. A witty, elegant and attractive woman, she had become acquainted with Cardinal de Rohan, a man with powerful influence at Court, and she managed to persuade the prelate that she was a close friend of the Queen.

Her ingenious scheme revolved around a magnificent necklace made by the crown jewellers, MM. Boemer and Bossange, on behalf of King Louis XV for his mistress Mme du Barry. However, the King died before it could be completed, and du Barry was exiled to England, so the necklace, which consisted of no fewer than 541 precious stones, was offered to the new King. Its price, 1,800,000 livres, was considered too high, and so the jewellers offered to make a valuable present to whoever could find a buyer.

Comtesse de la Motte wove her plot skilfully, telling the Cardinal that the Queen wanted to buy the necklace with her own money without the King's knowledge, and so desired the Cardinal to buy it on her behalf. She produced an authorisation forged by an ally named Marc-Antoine Retaux de Villette, purporting to be from the Queen, pledging payment to the jewellers.

Accordingly the necklace was given to the Cardinal, who in turn passed it over to the Comtesse for delivery to the Queen – except that it never reached the royal palace. Instead Jeanne de la Motte sold some of the gems, her husband taking the remaining stones to England, where he promptly disposed of 300 of them for £14,000: a veritable fortune in those days.

The jewellers, having received no payment, complained to the palace and enquiries were begun, with the result that all involved, including Jeanne, the forger Villette, and the Cardinal were put on trial. The latter dignitary was cleared of all blame but Villette was sentenced to be banished from the kingdom. Jeanne de la Motte was found guilty of initiating the plot, the sentence being that she should be whipped, branded on both shoulders with the letter 'V' (*voleuse*, thief), and imprisoned for life.

On hearing the sentence, Charles-Henri, the public executioner, sought clarification of that part which stipulated that the prisoner should be 'beaten and birched naked'; the ambiguous reply he was given was that he was to arrange the affair to take place as discreetly as possible, and to temper the severity of the sentence with humanity. The Comtesse was not aware of the sentence for, as was the judicial custom, the horrific details would not be disclosed to her until the actual day on which they were to be administered.

On 21 July 1786, the day of retribution, Charles-Henri was sent for and told that the prisoner had shown great displays of temper whilst in prison and would no doubt do so when informed of her sentence. Aware of his responsibilities and also that, rather than delegate it to an underling, he would have to administer the beating himself (the Comtesse being of noble blood), he realised that he would have to take all measures necessary to minimise any disturbance. Going to the prison, he told the gaoler's wife to inform the Comtesse that she was wanted in the corridor by her counsel. As soon as the prisoner left the cell, the executioner's assistants seized her arms as, on seeing them, she desperately tried to escape.

Charles-Henri was able to have a good look at his victim. He later wrote:

'She was rather small in stature . . . her expressive mouth was large and her eyes rather small. What was remarkable was the thickness and length of her hair and the whiteness of her skin, the smallness of her hands and her feet. She wore a silk déshabillé, striped brown and white, and covered with small nosegays of roses, and her head was covered with a small cap.'

Held firmly by the assistants and also surrounded by four police officers, the Comtesse trembled slightly as Charles-Henri said, 'We wish you to listen to your judgement, madame.' She was led to the hall, where the clerk proclaimed the verdict of guilty; as he did so, her eyes rolled in their sockets and she bit her lip, her hitherto pretty face a mask of fury. When the clerk came to the penalties her rage exploded into uncontrollable violence, a protracted struggle ensuing between her and her escorts.

Eventually overpowered, she was then tied up and carried down to the public courtyard where the scaffold awaited. Despite it being only six o'clock in the morning, a crowd of hundreds had gathered, and as her bonds were loosened, she ran towards the edge of the scaffold, a further frantic struggle taking place as, with an effort, they managed to strip the clothing from her and force her to lie down on the bench so that Charles-Henri could administer the beating.

A vivid description of what followed was portrayed in a journal written by Nicolas Ruault:

'Her whole body was revealed – her superb body, so exquisitely proportioned. At the flash of those white thighs and breasts, the rabble broke the stunned silence with whistles, catcalls and shouted obscenities. The prisoner slipped from his grasp, the executioner, branding iron in hand, had to follow her as she writhed and rolled across the paving stones of the courtyard. The delicate flesh sizzled under the red-hot iron. A light bluish vapour floated about her loosened hair. At that moment her entire body was seized with a convulsion so violent that the second letter 'V' was applied, not to her shoulder, but on her breast, her beautiful breast. Mme de la Motte's tortured body writhed in one last convulsive moment. Somehow she found strength enough to turn and sink her teeth into the executioner's shoulder, through the leather vest, to the flesh, bringing blood. Then she fainted.'

On recovering she was taken back by coach to the prison where, as the vehicle slowed down, she tried to throw herself under the wheels. In her cell she vainly tried once more to commit suicide by choking herself with a corner of her bed sheet. But her imprisonment lasted, not for life, as sentenced by the court, but for a brief ten months, for with the help of a sentry whom she bribed, she escaped to England disguised as a man and joined her husband in London, where she lived until her death in 1791.

In 1581, having penned seditious writings against Queen Elizabeth's proposed wedding plans, John Stubbs was sentenced to have the offending hand amputated. Just as the executioner positioned his meat cleaver on the joint of his victim's right wrist and raised the mallet to strike it, Stubbs, patriotic almost beyond belief, raised his hat with his other hand and, waving it in the air, shouted, 'God save the Queen!'

William Prynne, MP

The one thing a seventeenth-century author and Member of Parliament should never have done was offend members of the royal family, yet that was exactly what William Prynne did when he wrote a book criticising the theatrical profession because one person who loved acting was the Queen (Henrietta Maria) herself. Her husband, Charles I, was so furious that Prynne not only found himself serving twelve months in prison, but was also fined £5,000. Nor was that all, for what really hurt, in more ways than one, was that his sentence included being taken to Westminster where the public executioner removed one of his ears, and from thence to Cheapside, where the other was similarly amputated. Nor was the front of his face overlooked; an additional penalty required his nose to be slit down the centre. One hopes that he could see without the need for spectacles or pince-nez.

Far from being cowed into submission, the now no longer good-looking author proceeded to publish pamphlets criticising the bishops, hardly a wise move, for once again he was brought to trial. In court a member of the bench ordered the usher to expose the prisoner's scars. The official did so, pushing back Prynne's flowing locks to reveal a stub of gristle protruding from one side of his head.

'I thought that Mr Prynne had no ears at all,' quoth one of the judges, 'but methinks he hath ears after all!' Determined to deprive him of what little remained of his sole surviving aural organ, the court sentenced him to lose the stub, to be branded and imprisoned for life – and to be fined another £5,000.

So one fine day in 1637 the appropriately named Gregory Brandon heated two irons, 'S' and 'L', for Schismatic Libeller (heretical libeller) and applied them, one to each of William's cheeks. Unfortunately, in the heat of the moment he must have applied one iron upside down, and so had to burn it in again but at least was compassionate enough to ask the attendant surgeon to relieve the agony by applying a plaster. That having been done, Brandon continued to carry out the rest of the court's sentence by cutting off the residue of Prynne's ear; such a tricky bit of surgery that in so doing, he sliced off some of Prynne's cheek as well.

In 1635, while on his way to Tyburn and execution, Thomas Witherington said to the sheriff's deputy, 'I owe some money to the landlord of the Three Cups Inn a little further on and I'm afraid I'll be arrested for debt as I go past his door, so could we detour down Shoe Lane and Drury Lane so we don't get stopped at the inn, and so miss my appointment at Tyburn?'

The deputy, entering into the spirit of it, said that he couldn't alter the cart's route, but if they were stopped by the innkeeper, he, the deputy, would certainly go bail for Thomas. And so Witherington, 'not thinking he had such a good friend to stand by him in time of need, rode very contentedly to Tyburn.'

Burned at the Stake
Catherine Hayes

At dawn on 2 March 1726 a watchman found a man's head and a bloody bucket in a dock near Horseferry Road, Westminster. The head was taken to St Margaret's graveyard and, having been washed of the blood and dirt, it was displayed on a pole for three days for purposes of identification, and then placed in a large glass container full of spirits and shown to anyone who wished to see it. Three weeks later it was recognised as being that of a well-to-do man named John Hayes who lived in Chelsea, and suspicion fell on his wife Catherine. She was arrested and expressed a desire to see the head; on doing so she kissed the container and begged to have a lock of the content's hair.

While she was being interrogated, it was reported that the limbs and torso of a man had been found wrapped in blankets, lying in a pond in Marylebone Fields near the Farthing Pie House. Further enquiries elicited the fact that at a party in the Hayes' house, at which two other men had been present, a quarrel had started, during which Hayes was murdered with a hatchet by one of the men, Billings, whereupon Catherine had said, 'We must take off his head and make away with it, or it will betray us.' And she, together with Billings and the other man, Thomas Wood, cut it off with the latter's pocket knife, put it in a bucket and threw it into the Thames. Catherine had next suggested that the body should be put in a box, taken by coach to Marylebone, and there thrown into the pond. As it was too large for the box, she then suggested that it should be cut into pieces.

All three were confined in Newgate Prison and put on trial. Billings and Wood, found guilty of murder, were hanged, Billings' corpse being later gibbeted. Catherine Hayes was charged with Petty, or Petit, Treason, and accordingly sentenced to be burned to death (High Treason was the crime of plotting or causing the death of the sovereign, the 'leader' of the nation; the penalty was to be hanged, drawn and quartered. Petty Treason was that of causing the death of the husband, the 'leader' of the household, and if committed by his wife she was sentenced to be burned).

Catherine Hayes Decapitating Her Husband

Catherine Hayes was drawn on a sledge to Tyburn where she was chained to a stake, kindling and brushwood being piled around her. A rope around her neck was then passed through a hole in the stake, but it was reported that:

67

'at the very moment that the fire was put to the wood that was set round, the flames reached the offender before she was quite strangled by the hangman, for, the fire taking quick hold of the dry wood, and the wind being brisk, blew the smoke and blaze so full in the faces of the executioners, who were pulling on the rope, that they were obliged to let go their hold; more faggots were then piled on the woman, and in about three or four hours she was reduced to ashes.'

Saint Laurence, a Christian martyr, was sentenced to death by the Romans in AD 258. He was secured to a gridiron, a rectangular framework of narrow iron bars, and a fire was lighted beneath it. As the cruelly slow grilling took effect he, with defiant humour, called to the executioner, 'This side is roastyd enough, oh tyrant great; decide whether roasted or raw thou thinkest the better meat!'

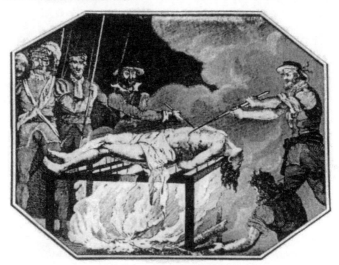

St Laurence Tortured On A Gridiron Over The Fire

Nicholas Ridley, Bishop of London

Man Burned At The Stake

Lady Jane Grey was proclaimed Queen in 1553, and Nicholas Ridley promptly denounced Princesses Mary and Elizabeth. When Jane was overthrown by Princess Mary, who then became Queen, he was committed to the Tower, deprived of his bishopric, declared a heretic and sentenced to be burned at the stake.

On 16 October 1555 he was taken to Oxford to suffer death by fire. A friend brought a bag of gunpowder and hung it round Ridley's neck. 'I will take it sent of God,' the Bishop said, although in that position the fire would have had to be well alight before it reached the explosive.

Unfortunately the branches had been stacked too thickly over the kindling and so the latter could not burst into flame; instead it continued to smoulder, white-hot, around his legs, prolonging his agony. 'I cannot burn!' he exclaimed. 'Lord have mercy on me, let the fire come to me, I cannot burn!'

With difficulty his brother-in-law threw some more wood on, but this only made matters worse, as it pressed down on the smouldering timber until another bystander seized a long pitchfork and lifted the faggots, so that the flames suddenly burst into an inferno. Whereupon Ridley forced himself into the heart of the fire, and the powder, igniting, did its deadly, albeit merciful, work.

At York in 1634 John Bartendale, an itinerant piper, was sentenced to death for robbery and duly hanged. After three-quarters of an hour the body was cut down and buried near the scaffold, but a passer-by later saw the earth moving and courageously dug the 'corpse' out. The muscular development in the throat and lungs brought about by the victim's profession having cheated the hangman, the judge ruled that, being legally dead, he

would not have to be hanged again – and Bartendale no doubt thanked
his lucky stars that he hadn't been a pianist!

John Hooper, Bishop of Gloucester

Another clergyman to suffer death in Oxford on the orders of
Queen Mary, John Hooper met his end outside the gates of the
college in which he used to teach those entering the priesthood.
As he knelt to pray, he was brought a box which contained the
Queen's Pardon and was told that if he renounced his religion,
he would be exonerated. He waved it away and proceeded to
obey the Sheriff's orders to remove his doublet, waistcoat and
hose.

He was then made to stand on a high stool with his back
against the stake, to which he was secured by an iron hoop which
was so tight that he had to press his stomach in with his hands
so that the executioner could fasten it. Upon the man
approaching with more hoops with which to encircle his neck
and ankles, he said they would not be necessary, exclaiming, 'I
am well assured I shall not trouble you; I doubt not God will
give me strength to abide the extremity of the fire without bands.'

The man appointed to kindle the fire then came to him and
requested his forgiveness, of whom he asked why he should
forgive him, since he knew of no offence he had committed
against him. 'Oh, sir' said the man, 'I am the man appointed to
make the fire.' Replied the bishop, 'Thou dost nothing to offend
me. God forgive thee thy sins and do thy office, I pray thee.'

He had been granted the concession of having three bladders,
each containing a pound of gunpowder, one hung between his
legs, the others beneath his armpits. Then, as described by an
eyewitness,

'command was given that the fire should be kindled, but it did not kindle speedily, but was some time before it took the reeds placed upon the faggots. At length it burnt about him, but the wind, having full strength in that place, it blew the flame from him, so that he was in a manner little more than touched by the fire.

Endeavours were then made to increase the flame, and then the bladders exploded, but did him little good, being so placed, and the wind having so much power. In this fire he exclaimed, 'Lord Jesus, have mercy upon me! Lord Jesus receive my soul!' And these were the last words he was heard to utter. But even when his face was completely black with the flames and his tongue swelled so that he could not speak, yet his lips went till they were shrunk to the gums; and he knocked his breast with his hands until one of his arms fell off, and then continued knocking with the other while the fat, water and blood dripped out at his finger ends.

Soon after, the whole lower part of his body being consumed, he fell over the iron that bound him, into the fire, amid the horrible cries and acclamations of the bloody crew that surrounded him. He was nearly three-quarters of an hour or more in the fire, as a lamb, patiently bearing the extremity thereof, neither moving forward or backward, but died as quietly as a child in his bed.'

At the execution of François Courvoisier for the murder of Lord William Russell in 1840, the famous novelist William Makepeace Thackeray was among the spectators, afterwards describing the surrounding windows as 'being full of quiet family parties of honest tradesmen, sipping tea, and moustached dandies squirting the throng below with brandy and water.'

The Electric Chair
William Kemmler

It was almost certain that if anything was going to go wrong, it would go wrong when William Kemmler, alias John Hart, who had murdered his mistress Tillie Zeigler with a hatchet, occupied the electric chair, for his was the baptism of the device which took place on 6 August 1890 in Auburn Prison, New York.

He, a short, black-bearded man, was introduced to the large body of physicians and scientists present to watch the proceedings and then strapped into the chair. The two electrodes were attached: one to the base of his spine, where his shirt and waistcoat had been split in readiness, the other to his shaven head. As the warden, Charles Durston, positioned the head electrode Kemmler shook his head a little, then said, 'I guess you'd better make it a little tighter, warden.' Durston readjusted it, then placed the mask over Kemmler's face, saying goodbye as he did so. 'Goodbye,' came the muffled reply.

The warden rapped twice on the door of the adjoining room and at the signal the executioner, concealed from those in the death chamber, threw the switch, sending 1,000 volts surging through the victim. After seventeen seconds, during which observers reported smelling burning clothes and charred flesh, the power was switched off but then disaster struck, for, as reported in the *New York World*:

> 'Suddenly the man's breast heaved. There was a straining at the straps which bound him . . . the man was alive! Warden, physicians, everybody lost their wits. There was a startled cry for the current to be switched on again. Signals, only half understood, were given to those in the next room at the switchboard. When they knew what had happened, they were prompt to act, and the switch handle could be heard as it was pulled back and forth, breaking the deadly current into jets.'

Taking no further chances, a second charge of 1,030 volts was allowed to flow through Kemmler's body for four minutes. Smoke was seen rising from the head electrode, and it was not until the body went limp that the current was switched off and Kemmler's lifeless body was removed from the chair.

Those on duty during an execution were always prepared to allow the victim to say a few final words, and doubtless expected a fervent prayer or protestation of innocence when murderer Charles Fithian, on taking his place in the electric chair, said he had a complaint to make. Granted permission, he then exclaimed, 'That soup I had for supper tonight was too hot!'

John Louis Evans

In April 1983 no fewer than three surges of current were needed to dispatch John Evans. During the first attempt, a defect was found with the wiring on the leg electrode: the wiring had burned right through, shorting the circuit. So, while Evans continued to sit in the chair, the technician hastily replaced the defective wiring, and once again the switch was thrown, but this time smoke was seen coming from the victim's mouth and left leg! Rather than delay any longer, two further applications of current were applied, Evans' body eventually sagging against its restraining straps, but ten minutes elapsed before he was confirmed dead by the prison doctor.

Not all criminals were overcome by the solemnity of the execution chamber. The Chicago gangster George Appel, on being strapped into the electric chair, exclaimed to the watching reporters, 'Well, folks, you'll soon see a baked Appel!'

Albert Fish

In 1928 Mr Budd of New York was contacted by a man offering to give his son a job. At the Budd's house the man, Albert Fish, also met his host's 10-year-old daughter Grace, and he offered to take the little girl to a birthday party being given by his sister. Somewhat reluctantly Mr Budd and his wife agreed. Grace never returned, vanishing without trace. Their overwhelming sense of loss continued for six years and was made even worse when they received an unsigned letter – later traced to Fish – which said, 'I came to your flat on 3 June 1928 and under the pretext of taking your daughter Grace to a birthday party at my sister's, I took her to an empty house in Westchester County and I choked her to death. I cut her up and ate a part of her flesh.'

Not long after writing this letter he was tracked down and arrested, much to the surprise of his unsuspecting neighbours to whom he had always seemed to be a quiet unassuming family man with six children, rather than the sado-masochistic pervert portrayed by some of the more sensational New York newspapers.

After further investigation and interrogation he was charged with the little girl's murder and he finally admitted his guilt, subsequently signing no fewer than six confessions in which he described in lurid detail what he had done; how he had first decapitated her, then cooked and cannibalised parts of her body. Police records showed that in addition to serving prison sentences for a number of different offences, he was also suspected of killing at least a dozen other children.

When put on trial, his defence lawyers attempted to show that Fish was not responsible for his actions; that he had been diagnosed as being addicted to self-mutilation, frequently inserting needles into the more sensitive parts of his body and had twice been held in psychiatric institutions for short periods.

But the jury was not convinced, and he was found guilty and sentenced to die by electrocution.

In January 1936 he was strapped into Sing Sing Prison's electric chair. The power was switched on and as the first charge surged through him, his body was seen to jerk and writhe desperately, the current failing to extinguish his life. A further attempt was made, and this time the officials present gave a sigh of relief as the doctor, after using his stethoscope, confirmed that Albert Fish had breathed his last. The cause of the first abortive attempt was never discovered, although many attributed it to the presence of twenty-nine needles in his body, some of them rusty, that were detected by the X-rays taken during the subsequent autopsy.

Serial killer Paul Jaworski passed the time in his cell by reading, appropriately enough, a serial story in a weekly magazine, and was disappointed when he realised he would be executed before the last instalment was published. 'Gee,' he exclaimed, 'it's tough not to know how it all ends!'

There was a happy ending to the event, however, if not for Jaworski himself, because the publishers, on hearing of the prisoner's dilemma, promptly sent him an advance copy of the final instalment.

Willie Francis
One can only pity this 15-year-old criminal, no matter how heinous his crime may have been, for the mental and physical suffering he endured when secured in Louisiana's electric chair in 1946. The switch was operated but despite the obvious surge of power, the victim was heard to gasp, 'Let me breathe.' The cause of his continued struggles could only be a lack of voltage, so it was turned off and then on again, only for those present to hear him exclaim, 'Take it off!'

The warden ordered the circuit to be disconnected and Francis to be released – from the chair but not his fate, for he was returned to his cell while the electrical problem was identified and rectified. This temporary and callous reprieve caused a public outcry, it being argued that a second execution would be a 'cruel and unusual punishment' under the Eighth Amendment of the American Constitution. However, the Supreme Court disagreed with this viewpoint and Willie was duly returned to the chair in the following year when everything worked without fail.

Emulating Bonny and Clyde, Irene Schroeder and Glenn Dague committed robberies across Pennsylvania until finally cornered by the police. During the shoot-out, Irene killed one of the policemen and both criminals were sentenced to die in the electric chair. Her companion was very much in her thoughts all the time she was in the condemned cell, and when she was asked by one of her guards whether she would like anything done for her on the morning of her execution, Irene replied, 'Yes, please tell them in the kitchen to fry Glenn's eggs on both sides. He likes them that way.'

Martin D. Loppy

Short but terrible was the account of the electrocution of murderer Martin Loppy in December 1891 at Sing Sing Prison. Half fainting, the condemned man had to be carried into the death chamber by the guards and held while being strapped in. No fewer than four separate surges of current were allowed to course through his body between intervals in which the electrodes had to be remoistened, but those present were shocked and horrified on becoming aware of the strong smell of charred flesh, and witnessing the victim's left eyeball being emitted from its socket on to his cheek, the fluid running down his face.

Sing Sing convict no. 69711 admitted his crimes but pleaded that he had robbed the rich for the benefit of the poor. Nothing unusual about that, but there certainly was in the manner in which he went to the execution chamber, for his request to walk there on his hands was granted. When finally strapped into the electric chair he said, 'Goodbye, Warden, old timer – now step on the gas!'

Charles E. McElvaine

McElvaine was sentenced to death for murdering a grocer and in February 1892 was escorted into Sing Sing Prison's death chamber holding a brass crucifix up in front of him. These were still early days in the evolution of delivering death by electrocution, and there was little doubt that the condemned man was petrified with fear as, seated in the chair, a leather visor was placed over his face, straps were tightened around his body, and he felt his hands suddenly immersed in large jars of salt water positioned beneath the sloping arms of the wooden chair. Next, the metal-wired cap was put on his shaven head and an electrode attached to his bare leg. All was ready. 'Let 'er go!' he exclaimed wildly and Davis, the executioner, operated the switch.

The first relay of current, lasting for fifty seconds, entered the jars and surged through his body via his arms, but when it was switched off it was very evident that either the method, the amount of voltage or the duration was incorrect, for from McElvaine came a moan, saliva pouring from his mouth. At this, the official in charge urgently exclaimed, 'Switch the current to the head and leg electrodes!'

As this was done, the condemned man stiffened in the chair, the now anticipated smell of acrid flesh and burnt hair filling the small chamber. Thirty-five seconds, seeming like minutes, passed before the current was eventually switched off and the doctor announced that the victim was dead – but the saltwater-filled jar method had proved disastrously ineffective, and was never used again.

Killer Michael Sclafoni was sentenced to death in 1930. Undaunted at the sight of the electric chair, he ran his fingers over one of the arms and shook his head. 'Dust!' he exclaimed and asked for a cloth. Given one, he proceeded to wipe the arms and the chair seat meticulously, then handed it back, commenting scornfully, 'They could at least have given a man about to die a clean chair!'

Ethel Rosenberg

The law does not differentiate between male and female victims, nor does high voltage, so when Ethel Rosenberg and her husband Julius were found guilty of being Communist spies, both perished in the electric chair on 19 June 1953.

Following her husband's execution – which apparently was accomplished without mishap – Ethel, wearing a green dress with polka dots, was escorted into Sing Sing's death chamber by two of her guards and seated in the chair. Seemingly calm and composed, she didn't flinch as the helmet fitted with the cathode element was placed over her head, its visor concealing her face from the observers present, and the other electrode was attached to the calf of her leg.

Executioner Joseph Francel delivered the first shock, followed by a further three. The sequel was reported in the *Sunday Dispatch* of 21 June:

> 'After the fourth shock, guards removed one of the two straps and the two doctors applied their stethoscopes. But they were not satisfied that she was dead. The executioner came from his switchboard in a small room ten feet from the chair. 'Want another?' he asked. The doctors nodded. Guards replaced the straps and for the fifth time electricity was applied.'

There was no mention of any signs of life after the first surge of electricity, and one would like to hope that that at least rendered her unconscious.

While Thomas Tobin was serving a prison sentence in Sing Sing Prison for robbery, it was decided to build a block of single cells, and Tobin, his other profession being that of a skilled mason, agreed to assist in the construction. He contrived to incorporate a short tunnel leading to a sewer which drained into the Hudson River, and he later used it to escape. He was eventually recaptured and completed his original sentence, but on his release in 1904 he committed further felonies, resulting in the death sentence. Back in Sing Sing he found himself in a cell which he instantly recognised. 'To think,' he exclaimed bitterly, 'that I should've built this place myself! I built my own tomb, that's what I did!'

William G. Taylor

A veritable series of errors combined to create total catastrophe when Taylor, sentenced to die for murdering a fellow inmate, was secured in the electric chair and the process began. As the first surge of current hit him his whole body straightened so violently that although the leg straps didn't break, the front of the chair itself did, coming apart from the rest of the structure. The power was switched off immediately, a guard procured a box and propped up the chair, and the doctor, assuming that the shock had proved fatal, routinely checked the victim's heartbeat – discovering, much to his surprise, that the man was still alive. At that, the warden gave the signal to the executioner to apply another surge of current. In his adjoining room, the official did so only to find that nothing happened, and on hastening to the powerhouse he discovered that the generator, overloaded by the amount of current it had to supply, had burnt out. Moreover there was no back-up or reserve equipment!

Faced with a totally unexpected situation, the warden had no alternative but to order that Taylor, now unconscious as a result of the first shock, be released from the chair and placed on the hospital trolley which had been brought into the death chamber.

Drugs were then administered to him to ensure that he didn't regain consciousness.

Meanwhile the prison electricians were frantically connecting long lengths of cable extending from their electricity sub-station to reach beyond the prison walls in order to obtain further electricity from the city's supply. Although they were not to know it, their haste wasn't necessary, for Taylor had already died on the trolley. When, an hour later, electricity supplies to the prison had been restored, Taylor's corpse was carried back to the chair, strapped in and subjected to a further thirty seconds of high voltage. For the law, of course, had to run its course in full.

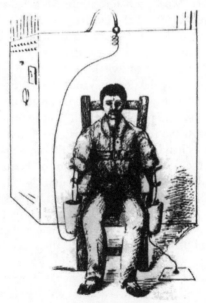

Early Electric Chair

The saying 'the condemned man ate a hearty supper' must have originated with one American prisoner in the 1930s, who ordered a Long Island duck, a can of peas and one pint of olives, all mixed into a brown stew with dumplings and boiled rice, together with tomato salad and four slices of bread. Then after finishing his sweet, which consisted of strawberry shortcake and a pint of vanilla ice-cream, he relaxed and smoked a few cigars. Following this feast he exclaimed, 'Right – I'm ready now to ride that thunderbolt, boys!'

Fred Van Warmer

Sentenced to death for the murder of his uncle on Christmas Eve 1901, it was two years before all appeals failed and Fred Van Warmer finally occupied the electric chair. The executioner, Robert Elliott, had sent two shocks of 1,700 volts coursing through the man's body for no less than two minutes, and was subsequently instructed to switch the power off. Having been pronounced dead by the doctor, Van Warmer's body was then released from the chair and carried into an adjoining room to await the routine autopsy. However, a passing guard happened to walk through the room and to his horror saw the 'corpse' move one of its hands, and one eyelid flicker. Shocked, he ran out to locate the doctor, calling as he did so, 'He moved! I saw him move! We've got to do something quickly!'

The warden and the other guards hastily reassembled and replaced the victim in the chair, where a further shock was administered; one so intense that when switched off, no doubt at all remained that Van Warmer had finally succumbed.

A later post-mortem revealed that Van Warmer's heart was larger than that of any previous occupant of the chair, a possibility that had to be taken into account when planning future executions.

A disabled felon sentenced to the electric chair had made a will in which he bequeathed his wooden leg to a newspaper reporter who had written some disparaging articles about him, adding in a codicil that he hoped the newsman would need it sometime!

Frank White

Frank White was a farm worker who had brutally murdered his employer and then hidden the body in a bale of hay. A violent prisoner while in jail, he refused all spiritual solace and was expected to resist as much as possible on being taken into the death chamber. However, the reverse was very much the case, for when escorted in, he was on the point of utter collapse and had to be supported by two guards. On seeing the chair he struggled wildly, shouting, 'Don't kill me! Don't do it! Don't do it!'

Somehow the guards got him into the chair and overpowered him long enough to strap him down. Further force had to be used to keep his leg still while the electrode was attached to his calf and, the other contact having been positioned on his head, the executioner operated the switch. Shock after shock of high voltage was applied, and after the fourth one, Dr Ulysses B. Stein, the physician on duty, checked with his stethoscope and announced, incredulously, that the man's heart was still beating.

The doctor then shakily resumed his seat in the front row of the gallery, but as the fifth shock was about to be administered, he fainted, collapsing onto the floor, and had to be carried to another room, where he soon recovered. During the subsequent two final shocks, many of the other onlookers were also understandably horrified by the gasps and gurgling noises coming from the victim, these sounds apparently being caused by the air escaping from his lungs.

During the uprising in the Vendée region of France, the revolutionary mayor wrote to his opposite number in Paris on 1 January 1794, saying, 'Our Holy Mother Guillotine works. Within three days she has shaven eleven monks, one former nun, a general, and a superb Englishman, six feet high, whose head was de trop. It is in the sack today.'

Firing Squad
Samuel and Malcolm McPherson and Farquar Shaw

This, a tragic episode in the history of the British Army, occurred in 1743 when 800 Scotsmen of Lord Sempill's Regiment (which later became the Black Watch) were inveigled south under the pretext of being reviewed by George II, only to suspect that they were actually to be sent to the then plague-ridden colonies of the West Indies and Africa. Encamped on Finchley Common, London, 110 of the men mutinied and set off to march in an orderly fashion back to Scotland. When the alarm was raised the Government sent three companies of dragoons (mounted soldiers) after them and offered a bounty of forty shillings to anyone who could capture a deserter. The pursuing soldiers caught up with the Scotsmen in Northamptonshire and escorted them back to London where they were imprisoned in the Tower. Court martials of three leaders followed, the two corporals, cousins Samuel and Malcolm McPherson, and Farquar Shaw, the piper (without such a musician, of course, no Scotsman would march anywhere!). In order to set an example, all three were sentenced 'to face death by musketry' (before a firing squad).

At 6 a.m. on 18 July 1743, the three condemned men knelt on planks positioned in front of a blank wall of the Royal Chapel of St Peter ad Vincula within the Tower. All their fellow deserters were drawn up in a wide arc in front of them, forced to watch the fate of their comrades, and encircling them to prevent any escapes, were 300 men of the regiment on duty in the Tower at the time, the 3rd Regiment of Foot which, ironically, later became the Scots Guards.

The three victims, wearing their shrouds under their uniforms, were ordered to pull their hats down over their faces; meanwhile the firing squad of eighteen men, six of whom were held in reserve, had been drawn up behind the Chapel. When the time came, as reported by General Williamson, Deputy Lieutenant of the Tower,

> 'they now advanced round the corner of the Chapple and with the least noise possible, their Muskets already being cocked for fear of the Click disturbing the Prisoners, Sergeant Major Ellison – who deserves a greatest commendation for taking this Precaution – waved a handkerchief as a signal to 'Present', and after a very short Pause, as they aimed four to a man, waved it a second time as a Signal to 'Fire'.'

All three men fell instantly backwards, apparently dead, but despite the squad having fired at more or less point-blank range, it demands a lot for soldiers to have to aim deliberately at fellow soldiers and pull the trigger, so it was hardly surprising that some bullets missed their targets. Shaw was seen to move his hand, so one of the six reserve members of the firing squad was ordered to advance and deliver the *coup de grâce* by shooting him through the head and Samuel McPherson had to be shot again through the ear.

The bodies were stripped to their shrouds and buried in an unmarked grave before the door of the Chapel, only yards from where Anne Boleyn and the other executed queens lie interred beneath the altar. The surviving deserters were duly dispatched to the colonies, few, if any, ever to return.

Admiral John Byng was court-martialled in 1757, charged with showing cowardice in the face of the enemy in that he failed to engage a French squadron near Minorca. His defence, that the French admiral had superior armament, was rejected and he was sentenced to death by firing squad. He was later visited by a friend who casually stood next to him and then

wondered aloud as to whom did he think was the taller. 'Why this ceremony?' asked Byng. 'I know what it means – let the man himself come and measure me for my coffin.'

When he faced the firing squad he requested that he should not be blindfolded, but was then told that it would only unnerve the soldiers and would distract their aim to see him looking at them. 'Oh, let it be done, then,' he conceded. 'If it wouldn't frighten them, it wouldn't frighten me.'

Edward J. Mares

Unlike the traditional method adopted by the military, in 1951 one American state employed five civilians as a firing squad and equipped them with brand new rifles. Their identities were concealed by selecting them in secret; moreover they were positioned behind a thick stone wall, their weapons protruding through gun ports. The condemned man was tied to a chair some little distance away with a heart-shaped target pinned to his chest. When the order was given, all the squad members fired with abysmal results; whether through humane reluctance or sheer incompetence, all the bullets struck the right-hand side of the victim's chest and death came with agonising slowness as Mares bled to death.

James Rodgers, robber and murderer, faced the firing squad in Utah in 1960. Upon being asked whether he had any last requests, he replied, 'Yes – a bullet-proof vest!'

Private Eddie Slovik

On 31 January 1945 in a little French village, a young army deserter was tied by his shoulders, knees and ankles by parachute cord to a six-inch square post to face a firing squad. He was Eddie Slovik, the only American soldier to be executed in that manner since 1864 and the only American soldier shot for desertion in World War II. Found guilty by court martial, his appeal rejected, summary justice had to be delivered, and seen to be delivered, as a warning to others.

Behind the post to which he had been secured was a stone wall, and in front of that was a parallel wall of thick heavy boards to act as a backstop; bullets fired from M-1 service rifles were capable of killing a man two miles away, and should any of the bullets miss the target and the post, they would penetrate the wooden boards rather than rebounding from the stone wall into the assembly of officers and paraded troops. A short crossbar had been nailed to the post at shoulder height to stop the corpse slipping down to the ground after the execution.

Twelve marksmen from Slovik's regiment had been selected to form the firing squad, a task which all understandably found distasteful; in fact one member reportedly asked his commanding officer whether he could avoid being a member of the detail, only to receive the dry reply, 'Not unless you want to take his place.' The men were issued with rifles, one being loaded with a blank round as a salve for the conscience, but this was hardly credible for there is little or no recoil with a blank, nor is its cartridge ejected afterwards, as is that of a live round.

After prayers had been said, a black cap was drawn down over Slovik's head and, in accordance with Army regulations, the order for his execution was read out. Eventually the dreaded sequence of orders was given, the major in charge shouting, 'Squad – Ready – Aim – FIRE!'

As the salvo of bullets found their mark, the man's body jolted, then slumped forward in the restraining cords. But he wasn't dead, witnesses reporting that they saw him struggle up at least twice. The regimental doctor, padre and other officers went forward to find that although all eleven bullets had struck Slovik, not one had pierced his heart. Checking with the stethoscope, the doctor established that breathing was still present, albeit shallowly, and the heartbeat was faint and fluctuating. Meanwhile each member of the firing squad was ordered to hold their rifles behind them out of their sight, so that they could be reloaded as before: eleven bullets plus one blank. When that time-consuming task had been completed, the officer in charge asked the doctor either to pronounce the man dead or to move away so that a second salvo could be fired, he and the squad no doubt feeling overwhelming relief as the medic said, 'The second volley won't be necessary – Private Slovik is dead.'

Perhaps the young soldier did lapse into unconsciousness when hit by the first shots; perhaps the terrible suspense-filled aftermath wouldn't have been necessary had a paper target been pinned over Slovik's heart; but that suggestion was rejected by the officer in charge as 'tending too much towards the theatrical.' What a pity.

Shortly before his execution on 29 October 1618 Sir Walter Raleigh met his barber, who said, 'Sir, we have not curled your hair this morning.' Raleigh replied jocularly, 'Let them comb it that shall have it!'

On reaching the place of execution on Tower Hill he saw his friend, Sir Hugh Ceeston, who complained that he had been prevented from accompanying him on the scaffold. 'Prithee, never fear,' exclaimed Raleigh, 'I shall have a place!'

Once there, he felt the edge of the axe and commented, 'This is a sharp medicine, but it will cure all diseases!'

Wallace Wilkerson

One man who did have a target over his heart was Wallace Wilkerson, in 1879. He was allowed to sit in a chair unbound while facing the muzzles of the firing squad's weapons. The orders were given to fire, then, as reported in the local newspaper, 'the instant the bullets struck, he got to his feet, partially turned and, taking two steps forward, fell on his left side onto the ground. On the instant of striking the ground he turned on his face, exclaiming, "My God! My God! They missed it!"' How wrong he was.

Found guilty of murdering his wife in 1910, Henry Thompson was sentenced to be hanged. While in the condemned cell he learned that the infamous wife-murderer Dr Crippen was to be hanged on the day following his execution. 'Ah, well,' he exclaimed. 'I'll be senior to him in the other shop!'

So unconcerned about his coming fate was he, that he commented to one of the prison warders guarding him that he expected his execution to be over quickly, adding 'Summat like that!' and then demonstrating it by standing on one of the chairs and leaping off.

Gas Chamber
John Redfern

As described earlier, small sacks of cyanide capsules are dropped into jars of sulphuric acid when the executioner rotates the rod to which they are attached, thereby creating the deadly fumes in gas chambers. But in 1943, when John Redfern was strapped into one of the chairs in the death chamber in Raleigh, North Carolina, the executioner operated the mechanism – but the capsules did not fall. He tried a second time, with the same negative result. While the victim waited, his nerves doubtless at breaking point, a frantic conference with the warden ensued, and a highly dangerous course of action was decided upon. Taking a desperate risk – and no doubt a deep breath – the warden opened the airtight door to the death chamber for the executioner to dash inside; free the sacks of capsules with one hand, then flee, the warden slamming the door behind him just in time as the noxious gases started to rise. And within minutes John Redfern was dead.

In 1992, after eating his last meal, which consisted of Kentucky Fried Chicken, two pizzas, a bag of jelly beans and a cola drink, murderer Robert Alton Harris entered the gas chamber saying, 'You can be a king or a street sweeper, but everybody dances with the Grim Reaper!'

Guillotine
M. Chalier

Although the guillotine was mechanically simple in its operation, great care had to be taken to ensure that both it and the scaffold on which it was mounted were on an even keel; the slightest diversion from the horizontal would result in the blade jamming in its grooves as it descended. M. Chalier found this out to his cost when, having been secured and lying flat on the plank with his neck held firmly in place by the lunette (the iron collar) between the two uprights, the blade was released. However, instead of descending at an ever-increasing rate, the blade fell more and more slowly, eventually coming to a halt, but not before making a superficial wound in the back of his neck.

The executioner, Ripert, desperately hauled the blade to the top again, hoping against hope that the first descent would have cleared whatever had initially obstructed it, but it was not to be – again the blade leisurely descended, only succeeding in deepening the wound rather more. At the executioner's bungling inefficiency, and their horror at the sight of the victim's ever-increasing suffering, the crowd's vociferous abuse now became more and more threatening and Ripert, his nerves rapidly approaching breaking point, tried twice more, then gave up; pulling a knife from his belt, he proceeded to decapitate the now badly mutilated M. Chalier. And if the expression 'to have a bad hair day' existed in revolutionary France, its meaning must have suddenly become clear when, on attempting to hold his victim's head on high, the wig came loose and he found that his victim was completely bald – so he had to display it to the crowd by holding it by the ears!

One cannot but admire the panache of the French aristocrat who, when offered a glass of rum to fortify him before being taken to the guillotine, waved it away with the comment, 'No thanks – I lose all sense of direction when I'm drunk!'

M. Lacoste

Another of the guillotine's many clients was M. Lacoste who, like M. Chalier, was also bald. This complicated matters for the assistant executioner, whose job it was to stretch the victim's neck ready for the blade by pulling on the hair or, failing that, the ears. But M. Lacoste had very small ears and so, although being held down by the iron collar, he managed to shake his head free of the assistant's grasp and sink his teeth into the man's hand just as the blade descended. The head duly fell; as usual the blood jetted all over the assistant's hands and legs; and he looked down into the basket to see the end joint of his severed thumb still gripped firmly between the teeth of the grimacing head.

Condemned to death in 1793 by the French Revolutionary Council, the Duc de Chatelat had previously attempted to commit suicide in his cell by cutting his veins with a piece of broken glass. On the scaffold, the executioner offered to dress his wounds to stop them bleeding.

'Don't bother,' the aristocrat said unconcernedly. 'I'll be losing the rest of it now.'

M. Collot

When one is to be guillotined, one does not expect to be delayed any longer than absolutely necessary – and certainly not all day. Similarly, when one is a spectator, one doesn't see why, just for voicing a small criticism or two, that one should be raked in to take part in the proceedings – and then lose one's own life into the bargain! Yet that is precisely what happened in Paris on 19 August 1792.

It all started when Monsieur de Paris, the executioner Charles-Henri Sanson, was ordered to behead a M. Collot, sentenced to death for forgery. The guillotine had been assembled on its usual site in the Place de Grève and as the horse-drawn cart containing the executioner and his victim arrived, they were greeted by a tremendous clamour from the large crowd waiting there, the outcry consisting of shouts of 'To the Carrousel!' The cart continued to advance, but a man seized the bridle and said that the will of the people was that the execution should take place, not there, but in the Place de Carrousel, opposite the palace of the late king, and that the executioner was to transfer his 'tools' there. After gaining the acquiescence of the Town Hall authorities, a procedure which took some considerable time, Sanson complied; the guillotine was dismantled and conveyed to the new location.

Meanwhile Collot, who up to now had been calm, began to struggle violently, and even more complications arose when it was discovered that most of the carpenters who had been paid to erect the guillotine on the first site and assist the executioner, had gone home on seeing it being moved away. However, members of the crowd, determined not to be cheated out of watching the execution, willingly, though amateurishly, assisted in the assembly of the machine on its new site.

By now it was nearly sunset and the felon, fearing appalling mistakes could be made in the half-light, begged that his execution might be adjourned until the next day, but the request, with its implication of further delay, was met with jeers of derision, the crowd's attitude becoming threatening. One of those nearest the scaffold, a beardless young man wearing the red cap of the Revolution suddenly stepped forward, shrieking that Sanson was a traitor and that he should taste the guillotine himself unless he 'operated' without further ado. The executioner explained that without his assistants, he could not dispatch the victim.

'You can find as much help as you require here,' exclaimed the man. 'The blood of aristocrats cements the happiness of the nation, and there is not one man in the crowd who is not ready to lend you a hand!'

A general cry of assent followed his words, but Sanson, noticing that despite their vocal willingness, those surrounding the scaffold had started to back away, hastened to accept the man's offer, and prevented him from re-joining his comrades.

All was then ready for the execution, but when Collot was led to the scaffold steps he refused to mount them, and Sanson had to carry the struggling man on to the boards. On seeing the dark outline of the guillotine, Collot's resistance became more desperate and he shrieked for mercy. The crowd grew silent, and the young 'volunteer' had by now turned very pale. At last, after a final struggle, the victim was strapped to the vertical plank, which was then pivoted horizontally so that his neck lay beneath the pendant blade, but his contortions were so violent that an assistant had to sit on him.

Sanson now told the young man that he could not furnish better proof of his patriotism than by taking a leading part in the execution, and he handed him the rope which released the blade. At his bidding the young man gave a tug; the blade fell, and the head dropped into the waiting basket. But this was not all, for of course it was essential to show the head to the multitude after decapitation, and the bloodthirsty onlookers were not slow in reminding Sanson that they were waiting. Determined to teach the zealous revolutionary a lesson, the executioner explained to him what he had to do. Reluctantly the young man lifted the head by the hair and advanced to the edge of the scaffold, but as he was raising his arm to display the bloody trophy to his triumphant comrades, he suddenly staggered and fell back. Charles-Henri, thinking that he had only fainted, went to his assistance – but the young man's violent emotions had proved too much for him and had brought on a heart attack: he was dead!

Having been deserted by her lover, beautiful blonde Manette Bonhourt took her revenge by becoming a mass murderer, killing nearly twenty men by using her allure, slipping drugs in their drinks and finally killing them with repeated hammer blows.

Even as Henri Sanson, the executioner, stared admiringly at her on the scaffold on 16 May 1808, she smiled and said provocatively, 'Don't you think it a pity to cut off a head as beautiful as mine?' Then, suddenly aware of the lustful expressions on the faces of the men clustered round the scaffold, she exclaimed furiously, 'Look at the vicious lot! They'd rather see me stripped for a whipping!'

Isabeau Herman

Not only was it essential that the guillotine be in full working order, the victim also had to be secured in the correct manner so that they were unable to move. This, regrettably, was not always the case, as evidenced by a report in a document in the French National Archives dated 27 May 1806:

'Among those executed on 14 April in Bruges was Isabeau Herman, a young girl twenty-two years old, whose beauty, youth and misfortune had attracted the sympathy of the onlookers, for on mounting the scaffold she had flung herself on her knees and begged the pardon of the crowd for the scandal she had caused by her irregular life.

The executioner, a very old man named Bongard, had failed to tie her legs to the bascule, and had left on her head her bonnet, in which her hair was gathered up. He had also omitted to cut her hair, and the movements of her head had caused some of her locks to fall on to the back of her neck.

When the blade fell, it did not sever her head, which remained full of life. She was horribly convulsed, and her legs fell off the board, leaving her in an indecent position. The executioner raised the blade a second time, but it proved unable to detach her head, until finally, at a third stroke, it was severed from her body. A howling mob besieged the scaffold; on every side, cries arose that the executioner must be stoned to death, and his life was only saved by the intervention of the armed police surrounding the scaffold.'

A journalist, while visiting the executioner Sanson, enquired about his daughter, to be informed that she had recently married a doctor. The visitor, believing that members of executioners' families could only marry those of others engaged in the same way of life, expressed his surprise, but the executioner replied, 'Eh, mon Dieu, let us look at things from a higher standpoint. To save a human body a surgeon is often obliged to sacrifice a human member, an arm or a leg! So when one of the members of the social body is gangrened, is it not the right thing to sacrifice that also?'

At that, the journalist exclaimed, 'But permit me to point out that there is a very great difference between the two sacrifices.'

The executioner smiled slowly, then said, 'Yes, Monsieur – in the size of the knife!'

Mme Thomas

This young French lady endeavoured to use her feminine wiles when escorted on to the scaffold on 23 January 1887 as, before an immense crowd of lascivious-minded spectators, she immediately started to remove all her clothing. With much difficulty, and assailed by a veritable barrage of lewd objections from the onlookers, the assistant executioner managed to restrain her and then had to drag her by the hair to the plank, where she was securely strapped down. He then went round to the other side of the machine, to hold her by the hair, writhing and screaming, as the blade fell.

That episode so appalled and upset Louis Deibler, the executioner, that he vowed he would never again execute a woman, and forthwith tendered his resignation; this, however, was neither accepted nor necessary, for after that occasion any death sentence passed on a woman in France was never carried out, except for some few cases during World War II.

When, on New Year's Eve 1793, executioner Charles-Henri Sanson went to the prison in order to escort General Biron to the guillotine, he found his quarry in the head turnkey's office, eating oysters with much gusto. On seeing the executioner the officer said, 'Please allow me to finish this last dozen oysters!'
Sanson replied, 'At your orders, sir.'
'No, morbleu,' exclaimed the general. 'It's just the other way about – I am at yours!' He leisurely continued his repast, remarking while he did so, that he would be arriving in the next world just in time to wish all his friends there a Happy New Year.

M. Laroque
One entry in the diary kept by the French executioner Charles-Henri Sanson describes how, on one occasion, a very unfortunate accident happened.

'Only one convict remained, all his companions having been executed before him. As he was being strapped down, my son Henri, who was attending to the baskets [exchanging those containing severed heads for empty ones] called to me and I went to him. Larivière, one of the assistants, had forgotten to re-raise the blade, so when the weigh-plank, the bascule, was rapidly lowered with the convict Laroque strapped to it, his face struck the edge of the blade, which was bloody. He uttered a terrible shriek. I ran up, lifted the plank, and hastened to raise the blade. The mob hissed us and threw stones at us.

In the evening Citizen Fouquier [his superior] severely reprimanded me. I deserved his blame, for I should have been in my usual place. Citizen Fouquier saw I was very sorry and dismissed me with more kindness than I expected.'

Sanson concluded that entry, as he always did, with that day's total: 'thirteen executions.'

In 1793 ex-Mayor of Paris, Jean Sylvain Bailly was sentenced to death by the Revolutionary Tribunal. The executioner, on climbing into the tumbrel with his victim, told an assistant to throw a coat over the man's shoulders, as the weather was chilly and wet. 'Why?' asked Bailly. 'Are you afraid I should catch a cold?'

On reaching the guillotine, the executioner discovered that the carpenters had forgotten some of the floorboards of the scaffold. The tumbrel party had to go back and collect the lengths of timber, the beams taking up so much space in the cart that both executioner and victim had to walk behind!

Eugen Wiedman

Public executions ceased in England in 1868, but continued in France until 1939, the last one there being that of Eugen Wiedman. Wiedman had a life-long criminal record of assault and armed robbery, and in 1937 changed his modus operandi by kidnapping Jean de Koven, an American dancing instructor, and holding her to ransom. But things went badly wrong for him and in desperation he murdered her, the remains not being found until four months later, buried beneath the steps of a villa in La Voulze. He subsequently went on a killing spree, killing four men and a woman, until eventually being captured during a shoot-out with the police. Charged with the multiple murders, he had little defence against the evidence produced in court, especially the long length of cloth he had forced down the dancer's throat, and that, together with other witnesses' testimonies, convinced the jury of his guilt, and he was sentenced to death, his execution to take place on 17 June 1939.

The guillotine was sited in the Place de Grève in Versailles, and in order to attract as little attention as possible the execution was scheduled for four o'clock in the morning. But the authorities failed to take into consideration the keen interest, indeed enthusiasm, of the public for such a spectacle. Hundreds of guillotine aficionados, determined to witness the felon's decapitation, started their vigil on the previous evening, filling the bars and cafés around the square and drinking throughout the night. Having had the hair at the back of his neck trimmed and his shirt collar cut away, and after smoking his last cigarette and sipping his last tot of rum, Wiedman arrived with his escort and, of course, Henri Desfourneaux, the executioner. The cheers of excitement reverberated around the square, followed by a hectic scramble as the crowd jostled to get a good viewpoint around the Widow Maker.

It was then that things started to go wrong. In order to minimise the publicity which the preparations would otherwise have attracted, no scaffold on which the guillotine would normally have been positioned had been erected, the killing machine itself therefore stood in the square at ground level. Consequently, the close proximity of the mob, many of them drunk, fighting to get as near as possible despite the police cordon, together with the sheer cacophony of noise, badly affected the usually well-drilled performance of Desfourneaux and his assistants. Strapping Wiedman to the bascule and quickly pivoting it into its horizontal position, it was then discovered that it was out of alignment with the lunette, the iron collar which should have gripped the victim's neck and held his head immovable. Not daring to waste time attempting to re-adjust the mechanism, and knowing that at all costs the man's neck had to be held beneath the blade, Desfourneaux did the only thing possible: he ordered his assistant to seize the felon's hair and ears, and pull his head forward.

Even as the man obeyed, the executioner released the blade; it descended rapidly, severing the head and sending the assistant reeling backwards, his clothes soaked with the blood which pumped from the torso to flood across the ground and into the gutters surrounding the guillotine.

So appalled were the authorities at such a shocking debacle and the barbaric behaviour of the spectators that a decree was hastily passed that all future executions were to take place in private behind prison walls.

When the French ex-Revolutionary leader Georges-Jacques Danton mounted the scaffold in 1794 to be guillotined, he surveyed the crowds contemptuously and said, 'Do not forget to show my head to the mob – they have not often seen one like it!'

Hanging
John Barns, William Mossman and Bernard Means

In 1785 these three men were convicted of serious crimes; Means and Barns for housebreaking and thieving, Mossman for theft. For some reason their leg-irons had been struck off the night before their execution, and none of them were prepared to go quietly to the scaffold. Under heavy escort they were led to the place of execution and in front of a large crowd – triple hangings were extremely popular among the townsfolk – they stood in line on the drop, the nooses were placed around their necks and the ropes tightened. And every rope broke! Amid pandemonium the trio were led down the steps again and made to sit there under heavy guard, to wait until prison officials returned from town with fresh supplies.

Wife-murderer William Borwick stood on York's scaffold and commented wryly that he hoped the rope was strong enough, because if it broke he would fall to the ground and be crippled for life.

James Bell

There were occasionally hangmen who were too tender-hearted for their own good. John Williams of Edinburgh, making his debut on the scaffold, was one who was so lachrymose that when ordered to hang murderer James Bell on 13 July 1835, he could not see through his tears to adjust the noose. The superintendent of the prison had to tell him to move aside and took over himself. Needless to say, the crowd did not appreciate hangmen who sympathised with their victims – why, they might even be tempted to shorten their sufferings, thereby depriving onlookers of their rightful entertainment – and Williams, dodging stones thrown by the crowd as he made his escape, decided that his first hanging was going to be his last, and he resigned the next day.

English hangman William Calcraft always rejected the accusation that he had actually put anyone to death. 'All I did,' he explained, perhaps tongue-in-cheek, 'was to make the preliminary arrangements required by law, as solemnly pronounced by an English judge – I placed the noose around the culprit's neck and then allowed him to execute himself by falling!'

William Bousfield

For many decades London's executions took place in public outside Newgate Prison and it was here, on 31 March 1856, that a particularly horrifying hanging took place. William Calcraft had gone to collect his victim from the condemned cell, to find him sitting on his bed, head slumped down on his chest, apparently oblivious to everything going on around him. The hangman was informed by one of the warders that Bousfield had already attempted to commit suicide by throwing himself in the fire in his cell but had been rescued by another warder, though not before their prisoner had sustained burns to his face and mouth. Weak and unable to stand upright after being pinioned, Bousfield was carried out to the scaffold seated in a chair, this being positioned on the drop beneath the beam to which the hangman proceeded to attach the rope and then noose his victim.

When the signal was given, the trapdoors opened, the chair fell through – but Bousfield didn't! Instead he began a desperate struggle to escape and, as reported in *The Times*:

'The sound of the falling drop had barely passed away when there was a shriek from the crowd, 'He's up again!' and, to the horror of everyone, it was found that the prisoner, by a powerful muscular effort, had drawn himself up completely to the level of the drop, that both his feet were resting upon the edge of it, and he was vainly endeavouring to raise his hands to the rope above his head. One of the officers immediately rushed upon the scaffold and pushed the man's feet from their hold, but in an instant, by a violent effort, he threw himself to the other side and again succeeded in getting both feet on the edge of the drop.

Calcraft, who had left the scaffold imagining that all was over, was called back; he seized the criminal, but it was with considerable difficulty that he forced him from the scaffold, and he was again suspended. The short relief the wretched man had obtained from the pressure of the rope by these desperate efforts had probably enabled him to respire, and to the astonishment of all the spectators, for the third time he succeeded in placing his feet upon the platform, and again his hands vainly attempted to reach the fatal cord.

Calcraft and two or three other men then again forced the wretched man's feet from their hold, and his legs were held down until the final struggle was over. In marked contrast, throughout this lugubrious event, the bells of the local churches were ringing merrily to celebrate the end of the Crimean War.'

A fearful moral for teetotallers to ponder is posed by the case of a saddler of Bawtry, Yorkshire, who was offered a fortifying drink of ale on his way to be hanged at York's Knavemire. Being abstemious, he refused the offer and the grim procession continued to the gallows, where he was duly hanged. But within a minute or two of the noose tightening, a messenger arrived with a reprieve – alas, too late. Now if the saddler had only paused to quaff his one for the road . . .

William Burke

William Burke

Contrary to popular belief, the notorious duo Burke and Hare were not body-snatchers. Instead of raiding cemeteries, digging up corpses and selling them to surgeons who desperately needed specimens for surgical demonstrations, Burke and Hare avoided getting their hands dirty and risking capture simply by finding old – living – people, plying them with drink, suffocating them, and then taking the bodies to the surgical schools. The total score of their victims is believed to have been about fifteen, and this would no doubt have increased had not the awful truth been discovered in 1828 when the naked, doubled-up body of an old woman was found hidden beneath some straw in a room of Hare's house by one of his lodgers, James Gray, who reported his gruesome find to the police. Both men were arrested, William Hare volunteering to give evidence against his fellow murderer, and because the authorities realised that without his testimony they had no case, the charge against him was withdrawn. The judge at the trial confirmed this, saying 'that whatever share you may have had in the transaction, if you now speak the truth, you can never afterwards be questioned in a court of justice.' Exonerated, Hare, understandably highly unpopular in his native city, was escorted across the border into England by the police. It is believed that, blinded by fellow workers while labouring in a lime-burning works, he eventually became a beggar, his patch being on the north side of Oxford Street, London.

Because of Hare's evidence there was never any doubt about Burke's guilt, and he was sentenced to death, the execution to take place on 28 January 1829. The local populace was in a state of high elation at the verdict, to put it mildly, and Burke had to be placed under strong guard lest an infuriated mob avenged themselves by taking the law into their own hands.

Shortly after noon on the previous day, preparations were begun at the site of the execution in Edinburgh's Lawnmarket. Stout poles were fixed in the street to support the chains by which the crowd would be kept back, and on this occasion the space was larger than usual. The work progressed, witnessed by a large crowd which gradually swelled in size as the excited locals came to watch the scaffold being built. As the night went on and the work approached completion, heavy rain fell, but the crowd showed no sign of diminishing and whenever an important part of the structure was placed in position they raised an approving cheer.

At about half past ten the frame of the gallows was brought to the spot, and its appearance was the signal for a tremendous shout. It was quickly positioned, for the workmen did their job with grim satisfaction, and when all was completed, so loud were the three cheers given by the spectators that the noise could be heard as far away as Princes Street. It was now about two o'clock in the morning and, wet and dismal though it was, those anxious to see Burke suffer for his crimes were beginning to take their places. Open spaces and stairways were quickly packed and by seven in the morning the vicinity of the scaffold was occupied by one of the densest crowds ever witnessed on the streets of Edinburgh, the numbers being estimated at 25,000. Every window giving a view of the place of execution had been bought up some days previously, the price varying from five to twenty shillings according to the excellence of the view; no mean amount of money for those times.

Meanwhile, in the prison, Burke had been visited by two Roman Catholic priests and two Protestant ministers, and he received their spiritual consolations calmly, without much apparent benefit, though he did lament his connections with the murders, to which he had confessed. Not that the prospect seemed to upset him to any great extent, for he slept soundly for the greater part of that Tuesday night and rose about five o'clock on the morning of execution day. He had been put in irons shortly after his conviction and now expressed a desire to have them struck off; they fell to the cell floor with a dull *clank*, to which Burke exclaimed, 'So may all my earthly chains fall!'

After praying for a while with one of the Roman Catholic priests, Burke was escorted to an adjoining room, but on the way he met Thomas Williams, the Edinburgh hangman, who accosted him in an unceremonious manner. Almost insolently Burke waved him away saying, 'I am not just ready for you yet!' but Williams followed him and started to pinion his victim. Burke submitted without protest, and when this was completed, he accepted the glass of wine offered him. Raising it to his lips, he looked around and gave his last toast, 'Farewell to all my friends!'

On his approach to the scaffold, the truly enormous crowd

sent up a loud shout and Burke was visibly shaken, as if afraid that the mob might break through the barriers and tear him to pieces, and he made haste to ascend the scaffold. Shouts of 'Choke him!' and 'No mercy, hang him!' came from all sides, but otherwise the crowd showed no sign of attacking, obviously content to leave it all to the Finisher of the Law, Thomas Williams. Burke looked around somewhat defiantly, then knelt and prayed with one of the priests, a move which infuriated the crowd, not because they thought he was beyond redemption – although they probably did – but because by kneeling, he had moved out of sight.

Ten minutes passed and the crowd was now getting extremely impatient. Burke, having finished his devotions, lifted the silk handkerchief upon which he had been kneeling and put it into his pocket. He glanced up at the gallows, and then stepped on to the drop with a firm step. The hangman proceeded to adjust the rope about his neck, and his confessor told him to say the Creed and when he came to the words 'Lord Jesus Christ', to give the signal and so die with the blessed name on his lips.

The shouts from the crowd continued, and the people, excited beyond reason, cried out 'Give him no rope!', 'Wash the blood from the land!' and 'You'll see Daft Jamie [one of his more pathetic victims] in a minute!'

Williams then tried to loosen Burke's neckerchief but found difficulty in doing so, and the condemned man said, 'The knot's behind.' Those were the only words he uttered in his last moments. The rope was then adjusted, a white cotton night-cap was put on his head and pulled down over his face, and he then began the recitation of the Creed. When he came to the holy name, he gave the signal, the bolt was drawn and the greatest murderer of his time swung on the gallows.

He fell the length of the rope with the multitude's fearsome yell ringing in his ears, and every time the body of the dying man gave a convulsive twitch – for the rope was much too short to bring instant death – the crowd cheered. An eyewitness said, 'He struggled a good deal and put out his legs as if to catch something with his feet [obviously Williams had either neglected or forgotten to strap the man's knees and ankles together] but some of the undertaker's men, who were down in the pit beneath the drop, seized his feet and sent him spinning round, a motion which continued until he was pulled up above the level of the scaffold boards.'

It was now a quarter past eight, and the body was allowed to hang until five minutes to nine, when Williams cut it down amid the gloating yells of the onlookers. They made a rush forward as if to lay hold of the corpse, but they were kept back by the strong force of police who lined the barriers. The hangman's assistants too, seemed to be affected by the general frenzy and a scramble took place among them for portions of the rope, shavings from the coffin, or anything that would serve as a souvenir of the great Burke and Hare tragedies. The body was then conveyed to the lock-up for the time being, and the vast crowd slowly dispersed.

But the mere extinguishing of the murderer's life was not enough to satisfy the bloodlust of the populace. Just as, centuries earlier, the severed head was held high so all could see that justice had been done and the felon had genuinely paid for his crimes against society, so even in the 'civilised' nineteenth century, everyone wanted to see and probably gloat over the mortal remains of William Burke, so the macabre circus sideshow had to continue. Accordingly, early the next day while the city was asleep, the corpse was transferred from the lock-up to the College where, just like Burke's victims, his body was to be dissected. The cadaver was laid out on a table and several eminent scientists and a sculptor, who took a cast of it for a bust, examined it before the students were allowed to enter and inspect it.

That afternoon Dr Munro gave a lecture on their new specimen and for that purpose the upper part of the skull was sawn off and the brain exposed. The brain was described as being unusually soft, but it was pointed out that a peculiar softness was by no means uncommon in criminals who had suffered the last penalty of the law. While this lecture was going on, a large number of students had assembled in the quadrangle of the College and were clamouring for admission. Those who were entitled to be present at the usual lecture time of one o'clock were to be given tickets, but there were so many students that it was difficult to issue them; at last the doors were thrown open and as many as possible of the young men, with or without tickets, were admitted.

The lecture was planned to last one hour but continued for twice that length; meanwhile the seething crowd of young men in the quadrangle had grown so unruly that the police had to be called to preserve order. Far from subduing the students, this only served to exasperate them and many made attempts to overpower the constables. Windows were broken and the police had to use their staves, many injuries thereby being inflicted. The Lord Provost and the College Baillie put in an appearance but hastily retreated, 'glad to retire with whole bones, under the abuse that was showered upon them.' Eventually the multitude were promised that good behaviour would result in fifty students at a time being allowed in and in this way order was restored, but not for long. The public in general then started to object to the students being allowed in, and they threatened that unless they too were permitted to enter, they would storm the College, seize the corpse and tear it to pieces. So further promises were given that the public would also be admitted, and this concession brought relative calm.

Those who witnessed the scene on that Friday, 30 January 1829, would never readily forget it. The authorities had made the most elaborate preparations for exhibiting Burke's body. It was placed naked on a black marble table in the anatomical theatre, and a passage was arranged to facilitate the movement of the viewers through the room.

The upper part of Burke's skull, which had been sawn off the previous day for the purpose of the lecture, had been replaced, and to the uninitiated it was unlikely that what was apparently a slight scar would be noticeable. Dr Leighton, one of the medical men present, observed that,

'the spectacle was sufficiently ghastly to satisfy the most epicurean appetite for horrors. There was as yet no sign of corruption or decay, so that the death pallor, as it contrasted with the black marble, showed strongly to the inquiring and often revolting eye; but the face had become more blue, and the shaved head, with marks of blood not entirely wiped off, gave effect to the grin into which the features had settled at the moment of death. However inviting to lovers of this kind of the picturesque, the broad chest that had lain with deadly pressure on so many victims [Burke's preferred method of suffocation while covering the victim's mouth], the large thighs and round calves, indicating so much power – but it was the face, embodying a petrified scowl, and the wide-staring eyes, so fixed and spectre-like, to which the attention was mostly directed.'

The doors of the anatomy theatre were thrown open at ten in the morning and from that hour until dusk the crowd streamed in along the narrow walkway, passing in front of the body at the rate, it was calculated, of sixty per minute, so that the total number who viewed it in this way was about 25,000. The crowd was composed mainly of men, although seven or eight women had also managed to gain entrance during the crush at the doors, but they were roughly handled by their male counterparts and had their clothing torn.

Dr Leighton went on:

'After the public display, Burke was cut up and put in pickle for the lecture-table. He was cut up in quarters, or rather, portions, salted, and put in barrels. At that time an old acquaintance of mine was assistant to the lecturing professor, and with him I frequently visited the dissecting room in the College. He showed me Burke's remains, and gave me the skin of his neck and of the right arm. These I had tanned, the neck brown, the arm white. The white was as pure as white kid, but as thick as sheepskin; and the brown was like brown tanned sheepskin. It was curious that the mark of the rope remained in the leather after being tanned. Of that neck leather I had a tobacco pouch made, and on the white leather of the right arm I got the artist Johnston to print the portraits of Burke and his wife, and Hare, which I gave to the noted antiquarian and collector of curiosities, Mr Fraser, and it was in one of his cases for many years.'

In the reign of George II, murder trials took place on Fridays, the condemned being allowed to repent during the Sunday before being hanged the following day. On being informed of that, one felon requested that his execution be postponed for a day or so 'because it was such a bad way of beginning the week!'

Martin Clench and James Mackley

These two men, condemned to die on the scaffold on 5 June 1797, were standing on the drop while receiving spiritual comfort from the Newgate Prison chaplain and a Roman Catholic priest, while hangman William Brunskill and his assistant were adjusting the nooses about the victims' necks. But someone had failed to check the bolts securing the trapdoors, and without warning they suddenly opened, plunging all six men into the yawning chasm, the two felons stopping abruptly as their nooses tightened, to die without absolution or blindfold. The other four, priests and executioners, plummeted on, to finish up in a struggling heap of arms and legs, profane oaths being emitted by at least two of them! The chaplain escaped with a few bruises, but the priest suffered severely when the two heavy executioners fell on top of him.

As reported in the Derby Mercury *of 1723: 'Last month Will Summers and John Tipping were executed for housebreaking. At the gallows the hangman was intoxicated with strong liquor and, believing there were three for execution, attempted to put one of the ropes round the parson's neck, and was with much difficulty prevented by the gaoler from doing so.'*

Newgate Gallows with Multiple Hangings

William Collier

George Smith of Dudley, the hangman who dispatched murderer William Collier outside Stafford Prison in January 1866, experienced a knotty problem when, having positioned the noose around Collier's neck, he stepped to one side and withdrew the bolts holding the trapdoors up.

But let *The Times* of 13 January take up the tale:

'The floor fell, but instead of the culprit's head being seen just above the scaffold boarding as expected, it altogether disappeared. There was a cry, 'The man's down! The rope's broken!' The powerful tug which resulted from the falling of the culprit through the scaffold floor had, in fact, been too much for the fastening by which the rope held to the beam. The intertwined threads became liberated, the knot slipped, and Collier fell to the ground.

For an instant there was dismay, both upon and below the scaffold. The executioner was for a moment bewildered. He ran down the steps and, beneath the platform, he found Collier upon his feet, but leaning against the side of the boarding, the cap still over his face and the rope round his neck. He seemed to be unconscious, and the hangman turned again, not knowing what to do.

A new rope, delivered to the prison belatedly the previous evening, was immediately brought to the scaffold in order that the prisoner could be hanged again. A second time did the halter sway to and fro in readiness, again did the priest, turnkeys, culprit and hangman appear in the sight of the crowd. Their reappearance [on the scaffold] was the signal for an outburst of popular indignation. The hoots and calls were repeated until the drop again fell.'

When Dick Hughes, a housebreaker, was going to execution in 1709, he happened to meet his wife at St Giles where, the cart stopping, she stepped

up to him and, whispering in his ear, said, 'My dear, who must supply the rope to hang you, we, or the Sheriff?' Her husband replied, 'The Sheriff, for who else is obliged to find him the tools to do his work?'

Replied his wife, 'Ah! I wish I had known so much before, 'twould have saved me tuppence, for I have been and bought one already.'

'Well, well,' said Dick. 'Perhaps it mayn't be lost, for it may serve for a second husband!'

Quoth his wife, 'Yes; with my usual luck in husbands, so it may!'

Hannah Dagoe

Hannah was born in Ireland but had settled in London where she had obtained employment working in the fruit and vegetable market in Covent Garden. She became acquainted with a poor but hard-working widow by the name of Eleanor Hussey who lived by herself in a small apartment, and the unscrupulous Irish girl broke in while Eleanor was absent and stripped the apartment of every article it contained. Blame immediately falling on her due to her friendship with the owner, her rooms were searched and, the evidence immediately being forthcoming, Hannah was brought to trial at the Old Bailey, found guilty and sentenced to death.

She was a strong masculine woman, the terror of her fellow prisoners, and had actually managed to stab one of the men who had given evidence against her. By contrast, when eventually en route in the cart to the Tyburn gallows she showed little concern over her rapidly approaching fate and paid no attention to the exhortations of the priest who accompanied her.

When the little convoy was halted beneath the gallows beam, however, somehow she got her hands and arms free and seized Thomas Turlis, the hangman; struggling wildly with him, she delivered a blow so violent that she nearly felled him. Shouting at the top of her voice, she dared him to hang her, declaring that come what may, he would not have her clothing afterwards, the garments to which he was entitled, and before he could restrain her, she tore off her clothes and threw them into the crowd, thereby adding considerably to their entertainment.

Hannah Dagoe En Route To Tyburn

During the hectic fight, it was reported that the escort of constables made no attempt to come to Turlis' assistance; one can hardly blame them for deciding not to take on this wildcat within the confines of a small cart. Eventually, Turlis, bruised and battered, managed to overpower his prisoner and get the rope round her neck, but as soon as she felt the rough fibres touch her skin and the noose start to tighten, she threw herself out of the cart with such force that she died instantly, perishing more mercifully in fact than had she been hanged in the usual way, writhing for an interminable length of time at the end of the rope.

Margaret Dickson

The *Newgate Calendar & Malefactors' Bloody Register*, published in 1891, devoted many pages to the crime and apparently miraculous recovery of Margaret Dickson after being hanged, though not without expressing a hint of Victorian doubt as to whether she really deserved it. Born early in the eighteenth century, Margaret Dickson was born in Musselburgh, about five miles from Edinburgh, and on reaching maturity she married a fisherman, by whom she had several children. Her husband was called up into the Navy and while he was away Margaret had an affair with a neighbour, by whom she became pregnant.

The *Calendar* explained:

'In those days it was the law in Scotland that a woman known to have been unchaste should sit in a distinguished [conspicuous] place in the church on three Sundays, to be publicly rebuked by the minister; and many poor infants have been destroyed because the mother dreaded this public exposure, particularly as many Scotch ladies went to church just to be witnesses of the frailty of another woman, but were never seen there on any other occasion.

Margaret's neighbours averred that she was with child, but this she constantly denied, though there was every appearance that might warrant the discrediting of what she had said. At length, however, she was delivered of a child; but it is uncertain whether it was born alive or not. Be that as it may, she was taken into custody and lodged in the gaol of Edinburgh. When her trial came on, several witnesses deposed that she had been frequently pregnant; others proved that there were signs of her having been delivered and that a new-born infant had been found dead near the place of her residence. The jury, giving credit to the evidence against her, brought in a verdict of guilty; in consequence of which she was doomed to suffer.'

In her favour it was subsequently reported that she behaved in a most penitent manner, confessed that she had been guilty of many sins and even admitted that she had been disloyal to her husband, but she steadfastly and constantly denied that she had murdered her child. She agreed that the fear of being exposed to the ridicule of her neighbours in the church had tempted her to deny that she was pregnant, and she said that when she went into labour, she was unable to summon the assistance of her neighbours; moreover she had lapsed into unconsciousness so that it was impossible she should know what became of the infant.

At the execution site she continued to protest her innocence, and expressed her sorrow for all her other sins. After being hanged for the requisite length of time her body was cut down and handed over to her friends, who put it in the coffin they had brought, and loaded it onto a handcart to be conveyed back to Musselburgh for burial. But, the weather being sultry, the cortège stopped at a village called Pepper-Mill, about two miles from Edinburgh, so that the mourners could refresh themselves at the local tavern. While they were drinking, one of them looked up to see the lid of the coffin move. Forcing himself, he cautiously and slowly slid the lid right back – whereupon Margaret Dickson immediately sat up and the rest of the company dropped their flagons and fled.

We have the *Calendar* to thank for describing what happened next: 'It happened that a person who was drinking in the public house had recollection enough to bleed her [a universal 'cure' for just about everything in those days]. In about an hour she was put to bed, and by the following morning she was so far recovered as to be able to walk to her own home.'

Others in that century who recovered after being hanged were almost invariably re-hanged, but by Scottish law, 'a person against whom the judgement of the Court has been executed can suffer no more in future, but is thenceforth totally exculpated; and it is likewise held that the marriage is dissolved by the execution of the convicted party; which indeed is consistent with the ideas that common sense would form on such an occasion.'

Half-Hanged Meg

So Margaret Dickson, having been convicted and executed, could not be prosecuted again, although the king's advocate did file a suit alleging failure of duty against the Sheriff, the official directly responsible for executing her, even though that gentleman subcontracted the job out to the public hangman.

For once we have a happy ending, for Margaret was reunited with her former spouse, thousands turning up to witness the unique spectacle of a legally dead woman remarrying her own widower! Given the name 'Half-hanged Meg', she later had several more children and obtained a job selling salt in Edinburgh marketplace, her second and final death not occurring until 1753.

In 1811 it was recorded that 'on Friday night, the evening before the execution of William Towneley at Gloucester, a reprieve for him was put into the post office at Hereford, addressed by mistake to the Under-Sheriff of Herefordshire instead of Gloucestershire; the letter was delivered to Messrs Bird and Wolloaston, Under Sheriffs for the County Hereford, about half past eleven on the following day. As soon as the importance of its contents were realised, a courier was humanely sent off with the utmost celerity to Gloucester, but the messenger arrived too late – the unfortunate man had been turned off twenty minutes before and was even then still suspended on the drop.'

William Duell

Under eye-catching headlines, the *London Magazine* of November 1740 gave a detailed account of a macabre incident which followed the hanging of 16-year-old William Duell for ravishing, robbing and murdering Sarah Griffin at Acton.

After being hanged by John Thrift (not the most dependable of hangmen), Duell's body was, in accordance with a law designed to deter other wrongdoers and also to provide specimens for medical students, brought to Surgeons' Hall to be anatomised,

> 'but after it had been stripped and laid on the board and one of the servants was washing him in order to be cut into, he perceived life in him, and found his breath to be coming quicker and quicker, on which a surgeon took some two ounces of blood from him. In two hours he was able to sit up in his chair and groaned very much and seemed in great agitation, but could not speak, tho' it was the opinion of most people that if he had been put in a warm bed and proper care taken, he would have come to

himself. The surgeons attributed his recovery to 'a full flow of vital blood which enabled his system to resist tightening of the veins.'

He was kept at Surgeons' Hall until twelve o'clock at night, the sheriff's officers, who were sent for on this extraordinary occasion, attending. He was then conveyed to Newgate Prison, to remain there until he is proved to be the very identical person who had been ordered for execution on 24 November [i.e. that Duell himself hadn't somehow escaped, his place having been taken by a substitute]. The next day he was in good health in Newgate, ate his victuals heartily, and asked for his mother. Great numbers of people resorted continually to see him. He did not recollect being hanged but said that he had been in a dream; that he had dreamt of Paradise, where an angel told him his sins were forgiven.'

At least he didn't 'go west' again (the direction from Newgate to Tyburn, hence the saying), for on appearing at the next session at the Old Bailey he was sentenced to be transported to the American colonies for life.

When sentenced to die by the guillotine, M. Moyse, having been found guilty of murdering one of his sons, exclaimed indignantly, 'What – would you execute the father of a family?'

David Evans

In 1829, the first year of his being appointed hangman, William Calcraft ran into considerable difficulties when he was ordered to travel to Carmarthen in Wales and hang David Evans, a young man found guilty of killing his sweetheart. On the scaffold it immediately became evident that a hangman's lot is not a happy one, for the crowd wasted no time in directing their abuse when, on operating the drop, the rope suddenly snapped and the victim fell to the boards, unhurt but not unnaturally in a severe state of shock. At the distressing sight the onlookers chorused, 'Shame! Let him go!' and the victim, staggering to his feet, gasped, 'I claim my liberty – you've hanged me once and you have no power or authority to hang me again!'

Nor was that all; as the crowd surged forward, crushing up against the scaffold, the gallows were seen to sway dangerously, threatening to come crashing down on those gathered below, and it was then discovered that the carpenter responsible had failed to secure the crossbeam sufficiently. Evans, now distraught, was heard to shout, 'It is against the law to hang me a second time!' But Calcraft, determined to impose his authority as executioner on the situation, said firmly, 'You are greatly mistaken. There is no such law as that, to let a man go if there is an accident and he is not properly hanged.' He clinched the argument by declaring, 'My warrant and my order are to hang you by the neck until you are dead. So up you go, and hang you must, until you are dead.' And with the assistance of two warders – and risking attack by the now infuriated mob – he proceeded to dispatch the still-protesting Evans into the next world.

Sentenced to death for murdering a policeman, James Murphy was held in York Castle. The night before his execution, while having his dinner, he was informed that the hangman was coming to have a look at him. Totally unperturbed, Murphy commented, 'Oh, show him in!' and continued to chew on a mutton bone as the executioner entered the cell.

On mounting the scaffold the following day, he noticed that the hangman was far from being calm and collected. To encourage him, Murphy exclaimed, 'Now then, you're trembling – don't be nervous, or you'll bungle the whole thing!'

Champ Ferguson

During the American Civil War the Confederates organised bands of their men to harass the enemy by attacking their lines of supplies and isolated units in much the same way as the British Army's Long Range Desert Group operated in North Africa in World War II. Most of the American guerrillas were well-trained and disciplined, but others were little more than thieves and murderers, one of their leaders being Champ Ferguson, a man known to have killed at least twenty-two people in cold blood, including an officer lying wounded in a hospital. On 24 May 1865 he was captured, court-martialled and found guilty, the death sentence being passed on him.

On 20 October everything had been prepared for his execution, which was to take place in the courtyard of the Penitentiary; sentries were on duty at the gates, soldiers paced the walls, and a hearse was parked within containing a coffin (despite Ferguson expressing a wish for one made of cherry wood, the one awaiting his body was of stained poplar). At ten o'clock it was taken out of the hearse and deposited in front of the gallows with its lid removed.

There were about three hundred spectators gathered around the scaffold. There had been a new crossbeam fitted and to the ring in the centre of it a four-strand manila rope had been attached, its strength having previously been tested with a two-hundred-pound weight. Ominously, the rope had been adjusted to permit just a two-foot drop.

The *Nashville Daily Press* published on the following day described the events as they unfolded:

'At twenty minutes past eleven Ferguson, his elbows and hands pinioned, was escorted out, to ascend the six steps which led up on to the scaffold, calmly and without assistance, apparently paying no heed to the coffin as he walked past it. He was dressed with scrupulous neatness in a black frock coat with vest and pants of the same material and black gloves and new gaiters.

The noose was then placed around his neck and for the first time he showed signs of emotion. His face flushed a deep scarlet, the perspiration broke forth profusely and his lips closed with a convulsive quiver. The realisation of his awful predicament seemed to have flashed over his mind in all its fullness, overpowering his fortitude. Colonel Shafter wiped the sweat away for him and the prisoner gradually recovered, then said, 'I want to be sent home to my family; I don't want to be buried in this soil.' After another pause he continued in an excited tone, 'Don't give me to the doctors. I don't want to be cut up here.' Colonel Shafter answered, 'You shan't, Mr Ferguson.'

A short silence followed and then the prisoner again said, 'I want to be put in that thing,' pointing to his coffin, 'and taken to White County, where I can have my family around me. If I had only had my way I wouldn't have been here. Whenever you are ready I am done. My last request is to be sent away with my wife.' The white cap was then drawn over his face. His last words were, 'O Lord, have mercy on me!'

As he uttered the last word, Detective Banville, at one blow of a hatchet, severed the rope which sustained the drop and the body fell some two feet with a heavy thud. He died easy, there being no death struggle as is often the case. Twice he slightly shrugged his shoulders and soon the desperate guerrilla whose crimes and cruelties had made his name a terror, was a corpse.

The first examination of the body took place thirteen minutes after the drop fell. The surgeon opened Ferguson's coat and vest and applied his ear to his chest. The heart was still beating forcibly. Five minutes subsequently, faint and indistinct murmurs of the heart were still heard. In four and a half minutes more, life was gone. The neck was not broken by the fall, but the rope had completely embedded itself in the front part of the neck, the knot having slipped to the rear. Considerable extravasation of blood occurred from the nostrils, as shown by the cap which covered his head.

At twenty-four minutes past twelve the body was cut down. The remains were placed in the coffin, the lid was screwed down and the spectators dispersed. In accordance with the opinion of the attending surgeons the immediate cause of death was cerebral apoplexy, the fall not being enough to break the neck. It is probable that he suffered little or none, though life was not extinct for some time, yet sensation ceased the moment the body dropped.'

But did it? One wonders, because his heart continued to beat for more than twenty minutes, whether he was still alive for that length of time.

In 1859, John Brown, the ardent American opponent of slavery (he whose body 'lies a-mouldering in the grave'), stood on the scaffold with the noose around his neck and then had to wait for ten minutes while the troops on parade marched and countermarched as they took up their correct formation. John Brown, on being asked by the gaoler whether he was tired, replied, 'No – but don't keep me waiting longer than necessary!'

Laurence Shirley, Earl Ferrers
In a more enlightened age this gentleman would have been diagnosed as having a serious mental deficiency, and confined somewhere where he could neither harm himself nor anyone else; as it was, he was simply put to death.

For the account of his crime we are once again indebted to the *Newgate Calendar & Malefactors' Bloody Register*, which described the Earl as being a man who was highly intelligent when sober, but a madman when drunk:

'Some oysters had been sent from London which, not proving good, his lordship directed one of the servants to swear that the carter had changed them, but the servant declined to take such an oath; the Earl flew on him in a rage, stabbed him in the breast with a knife, cut his head with a candlestick and kicked him in the groin with great severity. On another occasion, during a dispute with his brother and his wife, who were staying there, Lady Ferrers being absent from the room, the Earl ran upstairs with a large clasp-knife in his hand and asked a servant whom he met where his lady was. The man said, 'In her own room!' and, being directed to follow him thither, Lord Ferrers ordered him to load a brace of pistols with bullets. This order was complied with, but the servant, being apprehensive of mischief, declined to prime them, so the Earl did so himself. He then threatened that, if the man did not go immediately and shoot his brother, he would blow his, the servant's, brains out. Upon the servant hesitating, the Earl pulled the trigger of one pistol but it missed fire.

Earl Ferrers Shooting Mr Johnson His Steward

Hereupon the countess dropped to her knees and begged him to appease his passions, but in return he swore at her and threatened her destruction if she opposed him. The servant managed to escape from the room and warned the brother, who promptly roused his wife from her bed and they left the house, though it was then two o'clock in the morning.'

At this stage the really unfortunate victim enters the scene, a man named Johnson, who was steward (the keeper of accounts) to the household. The Earl had formed the opinion that Johnson was conspiring with the trustees over a contract for some coal mines, and had made up his mind to kill the man. And on Sunday 13 January 1760, he sent orders for Johnson to come up to the big house. When he arrived, the Earl took him into his own room and locked the door. Then, as graphically described in the *Calendar*,

'he produced a paper to him, purporting, as he said, to be a confession of his villainy, and required him to sign it. Johnson refused and expostulated, and his lordship, then drawing a pistol which he had charged and kept in his pocket for the purpose, presented it and bid him kneel down. The poor man then knelt down on one knee, but Lord Ferrers cried out, so loud as to be heard by one of the maids in the kitchen, 'Down on your other knee; declare that you have acted against Lord Ferrers; your time is come – you must die!' and then immediately fired.

The ball entered Johnson's body just below the last rib, yet he did not drop, but rose up, and expressed the sensations of a dying man both by his looks and by such broken sentences as are usually uttered in such situations. The report of the pistol having alarmed the women in the wash house, the Earl shouted, 'Who is there?' and ordered one of the women to send for one of the men and another to assist in getting Mr Johnson to bed. He then sent for Mr Kirkland the surgeon.

From the time the fact was committed, Lord Ferrers continued to drink porter till he became drunk; meanwhile the surgeon arrived and the Earl told him he had shot Johnson but believed he was more frightened than hurt; that he had intended to shoot him dead, for he was a villain and deserved to die; but 'now that I have spared his life, I desire you would do what you can for him.' My lord [Ferrers] at the time desired that he would not suffer himself to be seized, and declared that if anyone should attempt it, he would shoot him.'

The surgeon arranged for Johnson to be taken back to his house where he survived until nine o'clock the next morning, then expired.

A crowd of locals had meanwhile set out to arrest the Earl, and one of them, Curtis, saw him on the bowling-green.

'My lord was then armed with a blunderbuss, two or three pistols, and a dagger; but Curtis, being far from intimidated, marched up to him boldly, in spite of the blunderbuss, and my lord was so struck by the determined resolution that appeared in this brave fellow that he suffered him to seize him without making the least resistance; yet the minute he was in custody, declared that he had killed a villain, and gloried in it.'

From his home in Ashby de la Zouch the Earl was sent to Leicester Gaol and, a fortnight later, taken to London in his own coach and six horses under strong guard, where he arrived on 14 February 'dressed like a jockey, in a close riding-frock, jockey boots and cap, and a plain shirt. Being carried before the House of Lords, he was then committed to the Tower of London, having behaved, during the whole journey and at his commitment, with great calm and propriety. He was confined in the Round Tower near the drawbridge [now the Middle Tower, one in which the author was also often accommodated, though as a yeoman warder, not a prisoner!].'

On 16 April he was put on trial before the House of Lords and 'his lordship, in his defence, examined several witnesses to prove his insanity; none of whom proved such insanity as made him not accountable for his conduct.' Accordingly he was found guilty of murder and was sentenced to be hanged and then anatomised.

In the meantime a scaffold was erected under the gallows at Tyburn, and part of it, about a yard square, was raised eighteen inches or so above the rest of the floor, with a contrivance to sink down upon a signal being given, and the whole covered by a black cloth. The introduction of a platform on which the victim would stand was an innovative idea designed to replace the previous method whereby the felon stood in a horse-drawn cart, the rope around his or her neck, the steed then receiving a smart slap on its flanks.

About nine o'clock on the morning of 5 May, Lord Ferrers was brought out 'clad in a suit of light-coloured clothes, embroidered with silver, and said to be his wedding suit.' A long procession then departed for Tyburn, consisting of a very large contingent of constables, a party of horse-grenadiers and foot soldiers, and four coaches, with a hearse bringing up the rear. So great were the crowds lining the streets, all agog to see a real live lord going to execution, that it took the cavalcade almost three hours to cover the three miles or so to Tyburn.

Arriving there, he ascended the scaffold with the same composure and fortitude of mind he had possessed since leaving the Tower. After prayers he called for Tom Turlis, the executioner, who came to him and asked the Earl's forgiveness, to which his lordship replied, 'I freely forgive you, as I do all mankind, and hope myself to be forgiven.' His neck cloth was taken off and a white cap was put over his head. His arms were then bound with a black silk sash – for a common cord could not be used on a man of his rank – and the noose was placed round his neck. The raised stage started to sink but stopped after a few inches so that the victim's toes still touched its boards. An onlooker described how 'he suffered a little, having had time by their bungling to raise his cap, but the executioner pulled it down again, and they pulled on his legs so that he was soon out of pain and quite dead in four minutes.' (That 'raised-drop' method was not used again at Tyburn, but adapted, becoming the falling-trapdoor system later used at Newgate.)

After the regulation hour had elapsed, during which the Sheriffs and other officials took breakfast seated at one side of the scaffold, the body was cut down and placed in a coffin lined with white satin, his hat and the noose at his feet, then escorted by the Sheriffs in the same circus-like procession, to Surgeons' Hall, where it was anatomised. After being washed and laid out on an operating table before a large audience of medical men and students, 'a large incision was made from the neck to the bottom of the breast, and another across the throat; the lower part of the belly was laid open and the bowels taken away.' For the next three days it remained on display to large numbers of the public, who queued for hours to shuffle past the bier and gaze upon the final remains of Laurence Shirley, Earl Ferrers.

George O'Donnell, confined in the condemned cell at Winchester, commented to the warders guarding him that he hoped the hangman was not cross-eyed because he had met a cross-eyed man on the day he committed the murder, and seeing someone like that had always meant bad luck for him!

Elizabeth Godfrey

The executions on 22 February 1807 of three people found guilty of the murder of two men, John Cole Steel and Richard Prince, sparked off what was undoubtedly the most tragic calamity London's Newgate had ever experienced.

Two men, John Holloway and Owen Haggerty, had been sentenced to death for Steel's murder on Hounslow Heath, though much doubt existed over their culpability; the other victim, Richard Prince, had been stabbed to death by 34-year-old Elizabeth Godfrey; her weapon being a pocket knife implying that it was unpremeditated and that the charge should have been manslaughter, if that. Be that as it may, Elizabeth was sentenced to be hanged at the same time as Haggerty and Holloway, and when word got round the taverns and alleyways that not only was it going to be a triple hanging, but that one of them was a woman, thousands turned up at Newgate, some getting there as early as six o'clock in the morning.

What occurred on that day was dramatically described by a local chronicler:

'The crowd which assembled to witness the executions was unparalleled, being, according to the best calculation, nearly 40,000, and the fatal catastrophe which happened in consequence will cause this day long to be remembered. By eight o'clock not an inch of ground was unoccupied in view of the platform. The pressure of the crowd was such that, before the three malefactors appeared, numbers of persons were crying out in vain to escape from it; the attempts only tended to increase the confusion. Several females of low stature, who had been so imprudent as to venture amongst the mob, were in a dismal situation; their cries were terrible. Some, who could be no longer supported by the men, were suffered to fall and were trampled to death. This was also the case with several small men and boys. In all parts there continued cries of 'Murder! Murder!' particularly from the female part of the spectators and children, some of whom were seen expiring without the possibility of obtaining the least assistance, every one being employed in endeavours to save his own life.

A woman, who was so imprudent as to bring with her a child at the breast, was one of the number killed; whilst in the act of falling, she forced the child into the arms of the man nearest to her, requesting him in God's name to save its life; the man, finding it required all his exertion to preserve himself, threw the infant from him, but it was fortunately caught at a distance by another man who, finding it difficult to ensure its safety or his own, got rid of it in a similar way. The child was again caught by a person who contrived to struggle with it to a cart, under which he deposited it until the danger was over and the mob had dispersed. In other parts the pressure was so great that a horrible scene of confusion ensued, and seven persons lost their lives by suffocation alone. A cart, which was overloaded with spectators hoping to get a better view of the execution, broke down, and some of the persons falling from the vehicle were trampled underfoot and never recovered.'

Trapped on the scaffold by the screaming and panic-stricken crowd which surrounded it, their struggles shaking and rocking the very structure itself, hangman William Brunskill and his assistant John Langley had no alternative but to continue with their grim task, capping and noosing their three victims, the woman in particular shuddering with terror, both at the deafening riot taking place around the gallows and her own rapidly approaching execution. Brunskill operated the drop, but for once there were no triumphant cheers, no yells of abuse; the members of the chorus were too busy trying to save their own lives to take any notice of the three on the scaffold slowly losing theirs. It was reported, probably by someone on the very outskirts of the mêlée, that the two men seemed to die fairly quickly, but the woman was writhing and kicking for as long as half an hour afterwards. Although this would seem somewhat exaggerated, the very swaying of the scaffold under the immense pressure of the surging crowd about it might well have given that impression.

While it was possible to cut the ropes after the regulation hour had passed, it was out of the question to attempt to retrieve the bodies, since that entailed descending the scaffold steps into the swirling maelstrom of struggling humanity below and somehow getting beneath the platform, so the two executioners had to wait until the sheer cacophony of sound began to abate as the marshals and constables started to clear the streets.

As the officers began their grim task, it was reported that nearly one hundred people, young and old, lay dead or in a state of insensibility. A mother was seen carrying away the body of her dead boy, and a sailor boy who had been suffocated still grasped a bag in which he had some bread and cheese.

After the bodies of the dead had been stripped and washed, they were ranged round a ward in St Bartholomew's Hospital and laid out on the floor with sheets over them, their clothes as pillows beneath their heads and their faces uncovered. There was a rail down the centre of the room and the persons who were admitted to see the shocking spectacle went up one side and down the other. The entrances to the Hospital were beset, it was said, 'by mothers weeping for their sons! Wives for their husbands! And sisters for their brothers! Various individuals for their relatives and friends! And all to see John Holloway, Owen Haggerty and Elizabeth Godfrey swinging from a rope! Oh, what a tragedy!'

James Botting, the London hangman of the day, was once jeered at by some youths loitering at a street corner. When asked why he did not verbally

respond to their abuse, he commented drily, 'I never quarrel with my customers.'

Nor was he wrong in his judgment; ironically one of his tormentors, a man named Falkener, did qualify as one of his customers, being later found guilty of rape and, on 12 April 1817, had the dubious pleasure of meeting Botting again – on the scaffold.

Robert Goodale

It is doubtful whether Goodale would even have been caught, let alone hanged, had his fruit farm been supplied with mains water; as it was, a forty-foot-deep well provided water for his needs and those of neighbouring families. When, in 1885, the area was affected by drought and the well dried up, what should be found at the bottom but the body of Goodale's wife, Bathsheba, the cause of death being several severe blows to the head. There was little doubt about his guilt and so, having been sentenced to death, he was imprisoned in Norwich Gaol. There he was subsequently visited by the hangman, James Berry, who needed to make the usual routine preparations. On arrival Berry became aware of the nervous tension which was prevalent throughout the prison staff: not only had the governor ordered the operation of the gallows to be twice checked and tested, but one of the prison warders had told his colleagues that he had had nightmares in which the condemned man had not been hanged, but beheaded.

Berry did his best to ignore such prognostications, and got on with the job of deciding what length of drop to give the victim. It should be realised that while a short drop brought death by strangulation, it was not enough simply to give a much longer drop, since that would mean that the victim would be travelling too fast when the rope became taut, and so could be decapitated. When Berry's predecessor, William Marwood, a humane and thoughtful man, had taken over in 1874, he had devised a method of calculating the distance a victim should fall which would result in death coming quickly due to the severance of the spinal cord, by taking into account the person's age, weight, muscular development and similar factors. Berry had improved on this, basing his calculations on the assumption that an 'average' man weighing 14 stone would require a fall of eight feet, every half-stone lighter requiring two inches longer, depending on other concomitant features.

Now Goodale weighed over 15 stone and was of a flabby build, and Berry estimated that although by Marwood's criteria, Goodale should be given a drop of 7 feet 8 inches, he would err on the safe side and reduce this to just 5 feet 9 inches. Alas, events proved that he should have reduced the distance even further.

Execution day started badly. Goodale was determined not to go quietly, shouting for mercy and struggling wildly as Berry sought to pinion him, the hangman finally having to recourse to using lengths of cord to bind the man's wrists and arms instead of the more usual straps. The next problem was how to get him to the scaffold for, begging for mercy and almost collapsing with terror on seeing the gallows, he had to be half-dragged by four warders, and the situation was not helped at all when one of the warders suddenly fainted.

At last they positioned their man on the drop, holding him there while Berry pulled the white cap over his head and noosed him. The cataclysmic events of the ensuing few minutes are best described in Berry's own *Memoirs*:

'The whole of the arrangements were carried out in the usual manner and when I pulled the lever, the drop fell properly and the prisoner dropped out of sight. We were horrified, however, to see the rope suddenly jerk upwards, and for a moment I thought the noose had slipped from the culprit's head or that the rope had broken. But it was worse than that, for the jerk had severed the head entirely from the body and both had fallen to the bottom of the pit. Of course death was instantaneous, so that the poor fellow had not suffered in any way, but it was terrible to think that such a revolting thing could have occurred. We were all unnerved and shocked. The Governor, whose efforts to prevent any accident had kept his nerves at full strain, fairly broke down and wept.'

After descending into the pit and seeing the head, still in its white cap and covered in blood, lying some distance away from the huddled torso, Berry himself was almost overcome and had to be revived later.

At the subsequent inquest the Governor absolved Berry from all blame, confirming that the drop was not considered excessive. Dr Robinson, the prison surgeon, agreed, pointing out that although Goodale was tall and heavy, he had a very thin backbone; moreover his head had been cut off as if by a knife, and not torn off, and he concluded his evidence by saying, 'The sentence was that he should be hanged by the neck until he was dead. He was hanged and he is dead through being hanged.'

James Botting was executioner from 1817 to 1820 but had to retire after having a severe stroke. Confined to his bed, he suffered from hallucinations, probably the worst being the nightmare in which he saw all his 175 victims slowly marching past him, their faces concealed behind the mandatory white caps, their heads all tilted to the right.

'Damn their eyes!' he used to complain. 'If only they'd hold their heads up and take off their nightcaps, I wouldn't give a damn about any of them!'

Hangman Botting's Nightmare

Anne Greene

This young lady, just like Half-Hanged Meg Dickson mentioned earlier, cheated the gallows, but finished up in a much more bruised and battered condition.

The account of her seemingly miraculous recovery appeared in Dr Plot's *The Natural History of Oxfordshire*:

'In the year 1650 Anne Greene, a servant in the household of Sir Thomas Reed, was tried for the murder of her newborn child, and found guilty. She was executed in the castle yard at Oxford, on 14 December, where she hung for about half an hour, being pulled by the legs, sometimes so hard that the Under-sheriff forbade them, lest the rope break; and also struck on the breast, as she herself desired, by divers [several] of her friends, to reduce her suffering; and, after all, also had several strokes given her upon the stomach with the butt-end of a soldier's musket.

Being then cut down, she was put into a coffin and brought away to a house to be dissected; where, when they opened it, notwithstanding the rope still remained unloosened, and strait about her neck, they perceived her breast to rise; whereupon one Mason, a taylor, intending only an act of charity, set his foot upon her breast and belly, and, as some say, one Orum, a soldier, struck her again with the butt-end of his musket.

Notwithstanding all which, when the learned and ingenious Sir William Petty, the anatomy professor of the University, Dr Wallis and Dr Clarke, then president of Magdalen College and Vice-Chancellor of the University came to prepare the body for dissection, they perceived some small rattling in her throat; hereupon desisting from their former purpose, they presently used means for her recovery by opening a vein, laying her in a warm bed, and causing another woman to go into bed with her for warmth; also using divers remedies respecting her senselessness, insomuch that within fourteen hours she began to speak, and the next day she talked and prayed very heartily.

During the time of her recovering, the officers concerned in her execution would needs have had her away again to have completed it on her; but by the mediation of the worthy doctors and some other friends with the then Governor of the City, Colonel Kelsey, there was a guard put on her to hinder all further disturbances till he had sued out her pardon from the powers then in being; thousands of people in the meantime coming to see her, and magnifying the just providence of God in thus asserting her innocence.'

Anne made a complete recovery and was invited to recuperate in the countryside with friends who lived in Steeple Barton, and among her luggage loaded into the coach was a macabre memento of her ordeal – her coffin! She later married one of the local villagers, having three healthy children by him, and died some nine years later.

In 1780, executioner Ned Dennis was accused of being one of a mob attacking property in London during the Lord Gordon riots. Despite protests that he had been forced to join in, the court sentenced him to death. Dennis, mindful of the poverty of his family, begged the authorities to award the vacant executioner's job to his son 'a youth of sobriety and ability, who would be a credit to the profession.' The application was rejected, it being pointed out that should it be granted, the son would then have to hang his own father.

Dennis was subsequently reprieved in order to hang his fellow rioters.

Charles Julius Guiteau
Following the election of James Abram Garfield as the new American president in 1881, scores of job-seekers applied for jobs in the new administration, most being disappointed. Charles Guiteau put himself forward as a candidate for sundry important political posts, but was rejected out of hand. He was convinced that the President bore a grudge against him – so he shot him.

The assassin was born in 1841 in Freeport, Illinois, and studied law in Chicago. However, he switched to the other side of the law and took to swindling clients, but scenting further, more lucrative possibilities in the political world, he ingratiated himself with the committee members engaged in the 1880 election campaign of the Republican Party.

Upon the election of President Garfield, he travelled to Washington and, full of his own importance, considered that he merited being appointed to the Austrian Mission or the Paris Consulate-General. Not being awarded either of these prestigious posts, he came to the conclusion that his lack of success was due entirely to the opposition of the President and, learning that he was leaving Washington for a holiday in the North, Guiteau went to the railway station and lingered in the waiting room. As the President walked past, he fired his gun, seriously wounding his unsuspecting quarry.

The would-be assassin was immediately arrested and held in jail pending the result of the treatment being administered to the President. However the badly injured man lingered until 19 September and then died; whereupon Guiteau was put on trial charged with murder, found guilty and sentenced to death.

On 1 July 1882 the *New York Tribune* devoted many column inches to the killer's last hours:

'Guiteau ate a good breakfast and at ten o'clock took a bath in his cell. He then wrote the doggerel which he read on the scaffold. He was busy a good deal of his time copying his speech and poem, signing autographs on his pictures, and the like. As the hour of his execution approached he seemed to show more and more emotion and appeared to believe himself that he would need help at the gallows. During this time predictions were freely made among those waiting that he would collapse when the dreaded hour arrived and have to be carried to the gallows.

About 11 o'clock there was an unexpected sensation. His sister, Mrs Scoville, appeared at the door of the jail and demanded admission. She had no pass and the guards refused to let her in. Her other brother John went out to see her and the two met in the vestibule with a gaping crowd about them and every window in the jail which commanded a view of the scene was crowded with eager faces. She had flowers with her which she had brought to put on her brother's grave. She obviously had some excited notion that he would be safer and happier if she were at the execution, but General Crocker refused to admit her to the jail until it was all over, so she took up the flowers and walked through the crowd and over the dusty field to where some friends were in a carriage, to sit there until she should be called in to look on the body of her brother.

By 11.30 there was a crowd of 150 people scattered through the rotunda, chatting, laughing and smoking. As the hour of noon drew near, the crowd increased, both inside and outside. Within the rotunda the crowd now exceeded two hundred people and began to crystallise into two sections. One was massed about the opening in the corridor in which the gallows stood, in order to have the first chance in the rush which would follow close on the heels of the prisoner; the other was about the grating through which Guiteau would emerge from his cell. Near the entrance to the gallows corridor stood Officer Kearney, the good-natured and garrulous policeman who was the first to seize Guiteau after he had fired the fateful shot. He was busy today, telling his story and showing the card he took from the assassin's pocket and which first revealed his name.

At 11.45 a detachment of soldiers filed down the iron stairway at the back and drew themselves up into a single line stretching almost the full width of the rotunda. 'Attention,' came the order in low tones. 'Front face, ground arms,' and the muskets came down on the flagging with a heavy thud. The sound smote on the ears of the assassin in his cell and he fainted. Dr Hicks at once endeavoured to revive him by fanning him and soon brought him round but he was plainly full of terror, and weak. From that time until he was summoned to hear his death warrant read, he passed most of the time lying on his bed while Dr Hicks fanned him and spoke encouraging words to strengthen him for the final ordeal.

When the hands of the little wooden clock on the wall pointed to 12 there was a visible stir in the crowd and much comparing of watches. It is difficult to say just what the scene presented by the crowd was like – it was not exactly like a horse sale or an auction sale; the crowd was eager but cheerful and the only tension was that of curiosity.

While the crowd was thus eagerly waiting, the assassin sent out from his cell a characteristic request to have his boots blacked, which was of course granted.

Just before half past twelve word ran through the crowd that he had been crying, and predictions ran high that the last scene would be one of collapse and cowardice. The story had hardly travelled through the crowd when the procession appeared and it became known that the death warrant had been read in the cell. First came General Crocker and one of the guards, then Dr Hicks, followed by Guiteau with guards. The assassin's appearance sent a murmur of astonishment through the crowd. He was deadly pale and his eyes roved from side to side as he walked along, but his bearing was erect and firm and he seemed to wear a look of pride in his own courage and resolution.

Dr Hick's voice trembled as he uttered a few preparatory words and then he turned to Guiteau and held up an open Bible so that the assassin could read from it. The latter's voice was clear and loud, filling the whole corridor. There was not a tremor in it. He read a dozen verses in the same slow, unwavering voice. He read with a sing-song intonation, the same childish emphasis here and there, as he had at his trial, the same cheap actor's ranting pronunciation and the same curl of the upper lip. His body swayed from side to side in the easy manner of a speaker on any commonplace occasion and he looked away from the book at his audience at every other sentence.

After prayers had been said, Dr Hicks handed the book to

General Crocker and unfolded before the eyes of the pinioned man a sheet of foolscap.

'My dying prayer on the gallows,' said Guiteau in the same firm, loud voice, looking at the crowd, who were watching him with amazement. This, like the former reading, was a representation of all his mannerisms. He closed his eyes as he said, 'I tremble for the fate of my murderers.' His voice rose to a shout when he continued, 'This nation will go down in the blood,' and again, 'My murderers, from the executive to the hangman, will go to Hell.'

When he had finished reading his prayer he surveyed the crowd and said, still with a firm voice, 'I am now going to read some verses which are intended to indicate my feelings at the moment of leaving this world. If set to music they may be rendered more effective. The idea is that of a child babbling to his mama and papa. I wrote it this morning about ten o'clock.'

He then began to chant these verses in a doleful style; 'I am going to the Lordy, I am so glad, I am going to the Lordy, I am so glad. I am going to the Lordy, Glory, Hallelujah! Glory, Hallelujah! I am going to the Lordy.' Here Guiteau's voice failed and he bowed his head and broke into sobs. But he rallied a little and went on with his chant, 'I saved my party and my land, Glory, Hallelujah. But they have murdered me for it, and that is the reason I am going to the Lordy. Glory, Hallelujah! Glory, Hallelujah! I am going to the Lordy.'

Here again his feelings overcame him and he leaned his head on the shoulder of Dr Hicks and sobbed pitifully and then went on with two more verses. When he had finished his chant, Dr Hicks stepped forward and, laying his hand upon Guiteau's forehead, pronounced his benediction in a low voice.

The hangman, Strong, lifted the rope and put the noose in a calm, business-like way about Guiteau's neck and fitted it snugly in the manner of a tailor trying a coat on a customer. He turned it a little, this way and that, and looked it over with a critical eye. Guiteau's voice, coming with a ghostly sound through the black cap, was heard to cry, almost defiantly, as if with a last effort of the will, 'Glory, Hallelujah! Glory!' General Crocker then said, 'Are you ready?' in a low tone and, turning, waved his handkerchief at the cell window below.

He had hardly raised his hand before a sharp click of the bolts shooting back was heard and the trapdoors flew down and backwards in a flash. The rigid body of the assassin leaped into the gulf and jerked the rope as straight and as stiff as a bar of iron. There was no rebound, no swaying and no struggle beyond a quivering of the feet. The ghastly thing hung as still as a black bag of clothes.

Execution Of Charles Guiteau

The fall had hardly been made before a shrill and exulting cry rang through the jail from all the convicts in their cells, some of them murderers. It was a strange and thrilling sound as it echoed and re-echoed through the long corridors and was caught up by the waiting crowd outside, who knew what it meant and answered with cheers.

When the body had hung with the feet just touching the ground for over half an hour, it was lowered into the coffin which was waiting for it under the scaffold. The physicians decided at once that the neck had been broken. Those who desired could pass along the side of the scaffold and view the body. As the crowd filed past, John Guiteau fanned his dead brother's face to keep away the flies. At 1.40 p.m. the lid of the coffin was put in place and the body borne to the jail chapel, where the physicians who were to make the autopsy were assembled.'

The newspaper later struck a bizarre note:

'A visit to the jail will no doubt be a regular feature in the sightseeing of bridal couples hereafter. Several of them have been there and seemed to enjoy their visit. The guards and officers say it will probably be only a few days before the sightseers begin to stream in, and before another year is over, they expect to see the gallows hacked to pieces by the relic-hunters.'

In 1895 Sunday School Superintendent Theodore Durrant murdered two young women, Blanche Lamont and Minnie Williams, in San Francisco. Among the spectators at his execution in San Quentin Gaol was his father, his mother having to wait in a nearby room. Both parents were bitterly disappointed at having been refused permission by the authorities to film their son being hanged. After the execution the body was taken into an adjoining room and, it being assumed that the parents would be upset at the sight of their son's corpse, they were asked whether they would like a cup of tea. They accepted, but instead of tea, a full meal

145

arrived, so a table was set up a few feet from the coffin, and the father and mother sat down and ate a hearty meal. A newsman seated nearby reported to his editor that he overheard Mrs Durrant say brightly, 'Papa, give me some more of the roast!'

John Haley

Most hangmen took great care to bind their victims securely, which is more than can be said for the executioner in charge of John Haley when that felon was due to be hanged on the Tasmanian gallows. Not that Haley was innocent and so might have deserved a chance to escape his fate; on the contrary, for he had recently confessed to two murders in addition to the one with which he had been originally charged.

After the reverberations had died away following the parting of the trapdoors, and Haley swung, his upper half visible above the level of the surrounding boards, it was seen that somehow he had managed to get one pinioned arm free and was now scrabbling at his neck in a vain attempt to loosen the noose's stranglehold. The executioner didn't hesitate to take instant remedial action; raising one foot he proceeded to kick the victim's hand away. For a moment Haley's hand dropped, but then he raised it again; at that the hangman, obviously irritated by the murderer's refusal to die quietly and without further fuss, grabbed the rope and, while kicking out again at the man's hand and neck, started to shake the rope violently, uttering expletives as he did so.

Onlookers reported that Haley's struggles were frightful to behold, but eventually terminated, and the local newspaper included an article deploring the whole affair, saying that although the man was a self-confessed multiple murderer, such butchery on the part of the state was hardly compatible with the stage of civilisation a British colony might have expected to reach by 1861.

William Palmer, found guilty of poisoning his friend with strychnine and believed to have similarly disposed of at least a dozen others including his own wife and brother, was hanged in public outside Stafford Prison on 14 June 1856 before a crowd exceeding 50,000 spectators. On mounting the scaffold he became aware of the trapdoor on which he had been positioned. Testing it with his foot, he turned to the executioner, Smith of Dudley, and asked quizzically, 'Are you sure it's safe?'

Adam Hislop and William Wallace

Both Scotsmen were sentenced to death for robbery in 1785. It is likely that the latter man had been named after the Scots' national hero, and although he didn't suffer the same appalling fate as Sir William (who, after being captured by the English, was 'hanged, bowelled and quartered' in August 1305 at Smithfield, London), he still had a hard time of it. For, at the very moment the trapdoors opened beneath their feet, the ropes by which he and his companion were suspended suddenly broke, causing each man to lurch sideways in their descent, and instead of falling straight down through the aperture, came into violent contact with the edges of the platform. Both men also sustained further severe injuries on hitting the ground at the bottom of the pit, but there they had to lie until new ropes had been obtained, when they were once again assisted to mount the scaffold steps, once again to be noosed – and this time to be successfully dispatched.

Sentenced 'to be taken to the gyppet [gibbet] at Wigtown, Scotland, on 31 August 1709 and there hang until dead', Patrick Clanachan, the last man to be executed in that town, was being dragged on a hurdle en route

147

*to the gallows and, on seeing spectators running past to get a good place in
the market square, called out, 'Take your time, boys – there'll be no fun
till I get there!'*

Richard Johnson

Not all criminals were thick-witted or resigned to their fate, of
course; some were determined to stay alive at all costs and so
worked out ingenious methods by which they could cheat the
hangman. One such resourceful fellow was Richard Johnson.
The *Gentleman's Magazine* of April 1853 reported that:

> 'He was hanged at Shrewsbury on 3 October 1696, but it was
> found that after he had been suspended for a full half-hour, life
> was still not extinct. An inspection revealed a skilful arrangement
> consisting of cords under his clothing, and two hooks concealed
> by his flowing periwig, which prevented the noose from effecting
> strangulation. Johnson, in planning his scheme, must have had
> the connivance of the under-sheriff, of a concession to the effect
> that the customary removal of all clothes from the corpse before
> being placed in the coffin should, in his case, be dispensed with,
> but had overlooked the difficulty of simulating death in such
> circumstances and for any considerable length of time.'

His basic plan was excellent, and theoretically stood every chance
of succeeding; the hooks, positioned beneath the back of his
wig, not only prevented the noose from tightening around his
throat by catching over the rope, but being also connected to
the harness, took the weight of his body. And once placed in his
coffin fully clothed, thanks to the under-sheriff's cooperation,
he could possibly have escaped en route to the Surgeons' Hall
and subsequent dissection, and may even have arranged for
colleagues to create a disturbance so as to distract those charged
with escorting him thither.

Alas, ingenious he may have been, actor he wasn't; having to remain suspended, completely limp and motionless like a rag doll, was completely beyond his capabilities. Maybe he only half-stifled a cough behind his hood, or began to get cramp in his legs; whatever it was, it proved fatal in more ways than one, for after being cut down and his escape gear removed, the crowd received the bonus of a second item of entertainment as poor Richard was once more executed, this time decisively; after which his clothes were definitely removed before his corpse was deposited in his coffin.

In 1549 the Mayor of Bodmin, Cornwall, had taken part in an uprising, but so minimal was his participation that he was confident of an acquittal and this was further endorsed by the visit of Sir Anthony Kingston, who had invited himself to dine with the Mayor. The purpose of the visit, Sir Anthony explained, was to hang a man, and after the meal they adjourned to the newly constructed gallows.

'Think you it is strong enough?' queried his Lordship.

'It is indeed,' quoth the Mayor, only to recoil in shocked horror as Sir Anthony retorted, 'Well then, get you up – it's for you!'

Robert Johnston

There have been many horrendous blunders committed by hangmen in the past, but few can surpass the undiluted horror caused by the ineptitude and downright inefficiency of the Edinburgh executioner John Simpson when, on 30 December 1818, he had to hang Robert Johnston, aged 23, for the crime of robbery on the highway. *The Scotsman* vividly described how:

'the place of execution was in the midst of the most public place in the City, in the Lawnmarket. The gallows rested on the wall of the old Cathedral Church of St Giles, and under the gallows was

149

erected a scaffold, in the centre of which was a small quadrangular table on which Johnston stood, while Simpson attached a rope to his neck, the upper extremity of which was tied to the gallows.

When the criminal gave the fatal signal, it was intended that the table on which he stood should instantly drop to the level of the flooring of the scaffold, and leave him suspended [in much the same way as that used in the execution of Lord Ferrers in 1760]. But through the culpable negligence of those concerned in this operation, it really seemed as if the whole had been contrived to produce the shocking consequences which ensued. For, in the first place, the table, which seemed to be elevated only about eighteen inches above the level of the scaffold, was manifestly too low to admit of a sufficient length of rope between the neck and the gallows, unless it was intended to keep the unhappy man for a long time in torture, by making the rope quite tight before removing the table. In the next place, the table was so clumsily constructed that it could not be removed until some time after the signal.

Accordingly, nearly a minute elapsed after the signal was given before the table could be forced to drop, and after it was got down, the perpendicular fall was so short that the unhappy man's toes were still touching the surface, so that he remained half-standing, half-suspended, and struggling in the most dreadful manner.

It is impossible to find words to express the horror which pervaded the immense crowd assembled round this shocking spectacle, while one or two officials were at work with axes beneath the scaffold in a vain attempt to hew down a part of it beneath the feet of the criminal. Meanwhile the cries of horror from the populace continued to increase. Still the magistrates and others on the scaffold did nothing effectual; and it is hard to say how long this horrible scene might have lasted had not a person near the scaffold, who was struck by a policeman, cried out, 'Murder!' Those unaware of the circumstances of this assumed that the cry came from Johnston and, their feelings not able to bear further lacerations, went into action, a shower of stones taken from a loose pavement compelling the magistrates and police to retire in a moment.

The crowd then took possession of the scaffold, a genteelly dressed person cutting down the unhappy man and, after some time, they succeeded in restoring him to his senses. They then endeavoured to carry him off, and had proceeded some way along the High Street when the constables, who had abandoned their post on the scaffold, proceeded with their bludgeons to assail all the individuals who were around the near-dead man, of whom they at length recovered possession.

A spectacle now presented itself which equalled anything witnessed on the streets of Paris during the Revolution; the unhappy Johnston, half-alive, stripped of part of his clothes and his shirt turned up so that the whole of his naked back and the upper part of his body was exhibited, lay extended on the ground in the middle of the street in front of the police station. At last, after a considerable interval, some of the police officers, laying hold of the unfortunate man, dragged him trailing along the ground for about twenty paces, into their den, which is also the old Cathedral.

Johnston remained in the police station for about half an hour, where he was immediately attended to by a surgeon, who bled him in both arms and in the temporal vein, by which the half-suspended animation was restored; but the unfortunate man did not utter a word. In the meantime a military force consisting of men of the 88th Regiment arrived from the Castle under the direction of a magistrate. The soldiers, having been ordered to load with ball ammunition, were drawn across the street surrounding the police station and the place of execution.

It was now within thirteen minutes of four o'clock when the wretched Johnston was carried out of the police station to the scaffold. His clothes were thrown about him in such a way that he seemed half-naked, and while a number of men were around him, holding him up on the table and fastening the rope again about his neck, his clothes fell down in such a manner that decency would have been shocked, had it even been a spectacle of entertainment instead of an execution. Simpson then released his victim temporarily, in order to shorten the rope by taking a few turns round the hook above, then noosed Johnston again.

While they were adjusting his clothes, the unhappy man was left vibrating, upheld partly by the rope and partly by his feet on the table. At last the table was removed from beneath him, when, to the indescribable horror of every spectator, he was seen suspended with his face uncovered, and one of his hands broke loose from the cords with which it should have been tied, and his fingers could be seen straining to loosen the noose. Dreadful cries were then heard from every quarter. A chair was brought and, the hangman having mounted on it, disengaged by force the hand of the dying man from the rope. He then descended, leaving the man's face still uncovered and exhibiting a spectacle which no human eye should ever be compelled to behold. It was at length judged prudent to throw a napkin over the face of the struggling corpse.

The butchery, for it can be called nothing else, continued until twenty-three minutes past four o'clock, long after the street lamps were lighted for the night, and the moon and stars distinctly visible, and the execution continued until nearly half an hour after, controlled by the magistrate who had earlier summoned the military force. The soldiers, who had behaved throughout with the utmost propriety, remained at the spot until the body was cut down, and as it was then dusk, the crowd gradually dispersed.'

So appalled were the authorities at the fiasco that had taken place that Simpson was instantly dismissed; he moved to Perth, taking on the job of hangman there, but died soon afterwards, for which, no doubt, the criminal fraternity of that fair city were duly thankful.

In court in May 1896, Albert Milsom and Henry Fuller accused each other of the murder of their victim. Both were found guilty and continued their violent quarrel while being taken back to their cells. Later, on the scaffold, they were kept apart by having another murderer, John Seaman, positioned between them on the drop, and it is reported that Seaman's last words were, 'It's the first time in my life that I've ever been a bloody peacemaker!'

Captain Kidd

There may have been a small procession accompanying the infant William Kidd on his way to be christened at the local church; there was certainly a much more elaborate cavalcade on the day on which he died, the 23 May 1701. It assembled at Newgate Prison and was led by the Deputy Marshal of the Admiralty, carrying the Silver Oar, the symbol of the jurisdiction which that court held over all mariners. He was followed by the Marshal of the Admiralty, resplendent in his traditional uniform, riding in his official coach, his coachmen also clad in their distinctive livery, and behind them came the City of London marshals on horseback. The next vehicle, without which there would have been no need for such a parade of pomp and splendour, was far more commonplace but just as traditional, for, escorted by the sheriff's men, it had as passengers the City's hangman, the Newgate Ordinary – and the victim, pirate Captain Kidd.

The procession travelled to the bend of the River Thames at Wapping and Execution Dock, the site at the river's edge reserved for the execution of those who committed maritime crimes. Thousands packed every conceivable viewpoint, the riverside inns and jetties being jammed with spectators. Near to the shore, long lines of barges accommodated those who could afford such front row seats, while further out in the river, larger ships were moored, their decks and even their rigging swarming with sightseers, all eager to witness the death of such a notorious pirate.

In his younger days Captain Kidd had moved to New York, where he bought a small vessel and traded among the pirates who infested the area, although outwardly he professed to be such an honest and trustworthy man that the Earl of Bellamont, the Governor of New England and New York, employed him to assist in suppressing the pirates, and furthermore persuaded the authorities in London to raise £6,000 to subsidise such measures. Accordingly a vessel named *Adventure Galley* was fitted out and in 1695 Kidd and his crew sailed to Madeira, thence to Bonavista and St Jago, and eventually to Madagascar. Not encountering any of the pirate fraternity, he headed out into the Indian Ocean, where he stopped and captured the *Quedah Merchant*, a ship of 400 tons' burden, the master of which was an Englishman named Wright, the crew members being of Dutch, French, Moorish and African nationalities.

At that stage, reasoning that if he couldn't catch a pirate he might just as well become one himself, he sailed back to Madagascar, burnt the *Adventure Galley*, and divided the prize money (the cargo of his latest catch) proportionally between the members of his crew, depending on their rank, keeping forty shares for himself. Having transferred his spoils to another sloop, he disposed of the *Quedah Merchant* to a man named Bolton who, for whatever reason, decided to expose him to the authorities as a pirate; accordingly when Captain Kidd later sailed his sloop into Boston Harbour in 1699, Bolton was there – as were the governor's men, who promptly arrested him.

The following year he was sent, a prisoner under guard, to England, and appeared before the bar of the House of Commons, the members of which were investigating the grounds on which Kidd had been recruited in the first place as a 'pirate-catcher'. It was reported that 'the prisoner, who was in some degree intoxicated, made a very contemptible appearance in the House, on which a member, who had been one of the most earnest to have him examined, violently exclaimed, "This fellow! I thought he was a knave, but unfortunately he happens to be a fool likewise!"' He was committed for trial at the Old Bailey; his defence, that he had thought the *Quedah Merchant* was a pirate ship because it was manned by Moors, was rejected, there being no proof that the ship had ever committed any act of piracy, and he was sentenced to death.

Kidd went to his death drunk, a state which, as the Newgate Ordinary observed at the time, 'had so decomposed his mind that, now, it was in a very bad Frame.' But the frame that really did the damage was the structure to which the intoxicated Captain was secured – the gallows. Perhaps it was just as well that the felon had partaken of a few flagons of ale that day 'for the rope broke and he fell to the muddy foreshore again, but being immediately tied up again, the Ordinary again entreated him to prepare his soul to meet its important change. These exhortations appeared to have the wished-for effect, and he was left to swing, having professed his hopes of salvation through the merits of the Great Redeemer and his charity to the world.' Whether his hopes of salvation were ever granted, is not known; what is known however, is that his 'charity to the world' stopped short of informing the chaplain or anyone else where he had buried his piratical treasure.

After a suitable interval had elapsed and the tide was at its lowest, the executioner and his assistant cut the cadaver down and chained it to a wooden stake driven deep into the sands, its head and limbs to loll in rhythm with the waves of the next three high tides as a dire warning to the thousands of seamen who entered or left the City via the Thames each year.

Guilty of murdering one of his crew, Captain James Lowry was another who had been sentenced to be hanged at Execution Dock but, unlike that of Captain Kidd, his corpse was to be coated with tar, trussed in a tight-fitting 'suit' of iron straps, and suspended from a gibbet as a dire warning to all felonious mariners. He accepted the verdict of the court philosophically but on being visited by the blacksmith who had come to measure him for his new metallic outfit, he fell back on his bed in a dead faint, thereby making it easier for his 'tailor' to carry out his task. On regaining consciousness the Captain explained apologetically that it was not the fear of death that had upset him, but the disgrace of the public exposure!

Another condemned seafarer, William Jackson, awaiting execution in Newgate Prison in 1739, saw the blacksmith enter the condemned cell with his tape measure – and promptly dropped dead with fright.

John Henry George Lee

John Lee had been a servant in the household of an elderly lady, Miss Emma Anne Whitehead Keyse, who lived in Babbacombe on the Devon coast. Employing him had been an act of charity on her part, for when Lee was sentenced to prison for stealing from a previous employer, she had suggested to the authorities that rather than incarceration, it would help him correct his ways if he were to take a job in her house as footman and gardener. A fatal mistake, for on the night of 14 November 1884 one of the maids was woken by the smell of smoke and on venturing downstairs she found the dead and partially charred body of her mistress on the dining room floor. Shocked, she returned upstairs for help, there to be joined by Lee who, on seeing her faintness, supported her; she was later to discover that her nightdress bore traces of blood.

Investigations by the police revealed that Miss Keyse had been dealt a violent blow by a hatchet to the back of her head, her throat had been cut, and that at least five fires had been started in various rooms, paraffin oil having first been poured over the carpets and furniture. There were no signs of a forced entry, and in view of Lee's criminal record, he was arrested.

At the inquest, evidence was given regarding the blood found by the maid on her nightdress just after she had found her dead mistress; Lee refuted the allegation, saying that he had cut his arm on breaking open a window to allow the smoke to escape. What he apparently could not explain was the presence of hairs matching those of the dead woman found on his socks, and the fact that he had, in the recent past, uttered threats against her.

At his trial in Exeter Castle he appeared quite indifferent; so composed in fact that when the judge commented on it, he replied, 'Please, my lord, allow me to say that I am so calm because I trust in my Lord and He knows I am innocent.' However, despite the evidence being mainly circumstantial, the jury did not agree with him, and brought in a verdict of guilty.

Incarcerated in Exeter Gaol, he maintained his unconcerned attitude, and the atmosphere within the prison, tense at any time an execution was about to happen, grew even more jittery when the chaplain, the Revd John Pitkin, reported that Lee's warders had related how the prisoner had apparently dreamed of being on the scaffold, had heard the bolts drawn, but that the trapdoors remained immovable no fewer than three times.

At the appointed time on execution day, Lee, accompanied by the chaplain, the governor and other officials, was escorted from his cell to the coach house and calmly took his place on the drop, the soles of his feet bridging the slight gap between the doors. The hangman, Berry, strapped his legs together, slipped the white cap down over his head, noosed him, then stepped back and pulled the lever. But, other than a slight grinding sound, nothing happened. For a split second, no one moved; then Berry jerked the lever again – still nothing.

Half-Hanged Lee On The Drop

Desperation starting to creep in, he stamped on the trapdoor nearest to him, again with no results. The warders present then risked a rapid descent by also adding their weight to the doors, but the hazard was non-existent, for the drop remained closed. All this time, about five minutes or so, Lee stood immovable where he had been positioned, and one wonders whether he was unconcerned because, having been so convinced, or mentally programmed by his dream, he just knew beyond any shadow of a doubt that he was not going to hang.

Berry, realising that whatever serious defect was causing this appalling problem could not be rectified with his victim standing there, removed the noose and the cap, Lee then being led into a nearby room. Watched by those on the scaffold, the hangman then proceeded to operate the drop again – to find that it worked perfectly. So Lee was brought back in and readied once more for his execution. Berry then pulled the lever so hard that he bent it – to no avail, for once again, the drop didn't.

An air of approaching panic now permeating the execution chamber, the chaplain escorted Lee back to the side room while the hangman and a carpenter got to work with planes and an axe, slicing pieces of wood from the sides of the doors until the gap between them and the surrounding boards was so wide that nothing could have caused them to jam. Some secondary catches were also removed with a crowbar, and then Lee was brought in again.

To all present – not only those in an official capacity on the scaffold but also the group of journalists and other witnesses who had been granted permission to watch through a window in the shed – it must have all seemed like some fearful nightmare, as if everyone, victim and onlookers, were trapped in a repetitive cycle of horror, and when Berry pulled the lever again, with totally negative results, the trauma proved too much for some, the chaplain being on the verge of collapse, some witnesses in tears.

At that point, the governor took the only humane action possible under the circumstances, authorising that the execution be halted and that the Home Secretary should be immediately notified.

Lee, still unruffled, was returned to his cell, so cool and collected in fact that, on hearing that Berry could not face eating the breakfast prepared for him, the now ex-condemned man volunteered to eat it instead, and sat down to a repast of chicken, potatoes, muffins and cake, together with a large pot of tea. Meanwhile at the Home Office, rapid decisions were made, and in consequence the Home Secretary ordered that Lee's sentence should be commuted on humanitarian grounds to penal servitude for life: twenty years' imprisonment.

He was released in 1907, at the age of forty-three, but after a few years in London he immigrated to America, unfortunately nothing more being heard of him, for it would have been interesting to learn whether he had any theories concerning his good fortune, any premonition, or did he simply accept that, being innocent, it was his rightful due?

Dr Thomas Neill Cream poisoned his mistress' husband with strychnine and later murdered several prostitutes in the same manner. As these were the same class of victims who had been killed in London and 'surgically' mutilated only a few years earlier, great attention was paid when, on 15 November 1892, he was led on to the scaffold. There, hangman Billington hooded and noosed his victim, then stepped back and pulled the lever which operated the drop. Just as he did so he heard Cream say, 'I am Jack the . . .' He never finished the sentence but plummeted into the pit below as the rope tightened.

The executioner said afterwards, 'If I had only known he was going to

speak I would have waited for the end of the sentence; I am certain that Neill Cream and Jack the Ripper were one and the same man.'

Michael Magee

Michael Magee was sentenced to death in Australia for trying to deprive the township of its sheriff, and his execution provided entertainment for the large crowds which travelled eastwards from Adelaide to gather under the gum trees which lined the banks of the river Torrens.

To preserve his anonymity in case the would-be murderer had any vengefully minded confederates, the hangman wore a mask, and after he had considerately allowed his victim to apologise to the crowd for his sins, he noosed him, pulled the cap over his face, and then lashed the flanks of the steeds harnessed to the cart in which, in old English style, the felon stood. Unlike the English horses, however, these particular Australian animals were in no hurry to go anywhere; they ambled forward so leisurely that Magee slithered off a fraction at a time, the noose tightening equally slowly around his throat. Worse was to follow, the onlookers gasping in horror as the felon, the badly tied cords round his wrists coming undone in his struggles, managed to raise his hands and grasp the rope above him in attempt to take his weight off it. As if on a turnspit, he spun round and round, the efforts of his scrabbling fingers allowing him just sufficient breath to cry chokingly, 'Oh, God! Oh, Christ, save me!'

His efforts to free himself came to a sudden end when the hangman, emulating his English counterparts, clutched his victim to him and raised his own feet off the boards, their combined weight on the rope bringing death to the felon – but not until thirteen minutes had elapsed.

John Paynes, guilty of murdering six people, was taken to Tyburn on 19 July 1694. Before he was hanged 'he kickt the prison chaplain out of the cart and pulled his own shoes off, sayeing he'd contradict the old proverb and not die in them.'

Ewan MacDonald

It was recorded in the *Loval Historians' Table Book* that Ewan MacDonald, a 19-year-old soldier in General Guise's Regiment stationed at Newcastle on Tyne, was sentenced to death for murder, the execution to be carried out on 28 September 1752. On the scaffold he struggled frantically and even tried to throw the executioner off the ladder, but sheer weight of numbers triumphed and the condemned man was eventually suspended from the beam. Some little time later he was cut down, his body being taken to Surgeons' Hall and placed on the slab ready to be dissected. However, the surgeons were suddenly called away to attend to an emergency in the local hospital, only to find, on their return, that the specimen they were looking forward to dissecting was in fact sitting upright on the slab, a dazed expression on his face! Realising his whereabouts – and his likely fate – he desperately started to beg for mercy, but as quoted in the *Table Book*, 'a young surgeon, refusing to be disappointed of a dissection opportunity, seized a wooden mall [mallet] and struck him on the head, the blow proving too much for MacDonald, who finally expired this time. The identical mall is said to be often produced and shown to new surgeons, but whether as a curio or warning is not known.'

Found guilty of being involved in the shooting of Thomas Thynne with a blunderbuss in 1681, Christopher Vratz was sentenced to be hanged. On the scaffold he told a friend that, 'he did not value dying all of a rush

like this, and hoped and believed that God would deal with him like a gentleman.'

William Gordan

A laudable but failed attempt to cheat the gallows was undertaken, to employ a most appropriate word, by one William Gordan. The blunder however, was not committed by the hangman, but by a surgeon, Mr Chovet, who had the novel but mistaken notion that he could ensure Gordan's continued existence after being hanged. Gordan already had a criminal record as a career highwayman, and had one time been charged with robbing the Fishmongers' Company in London, but friends in Ireland conveniently provided him with an alibi for the date in question and so he was acquitted.

He may have been a successful highwayman, but he was riding for a fall when, while looking for likely victims on one of his favourite beats (the lonely road between Knightsbridge and Hyde Park Corner) he held up a lawyer, Mr Peters, who, on hearing the challenge, 'Your money or your life!' hesitated not, but decided that he preferred to go on living, albeit broke, and so obeyed Gordan, handing over not only his watch and ring, but also his hat and wig. Alas for the highwayman, he got drunk before disposing of the loot and, being arrested, any defence proved a waste of the court's time. Consequently the judge appeared on the bench, wearing his black cap, and Gordan later appeared on the scaffold wearing his white one.

The felon was to be hanged at the Old Bailey on 7 April 1733, together with three other criminals and a woman, Elizabeth Arden, who had been found guilty of robbing her mother. Elizabeth, however, 'pleaded her belly' and, it being confirmed that she was indeed pregnant, was instead transported to the penal colonies for fourteen years.

Now Gordan, it appears, had hatched a cunning plan with Mr Chovet to cheat the rope. The surgeon had been experimenting on dogs and was confident that by making an incision in the lower part of Gordan's throat, air would still reach his lungs even though the constriction of the noose immediately below his chin would prevent him breathing in via his nose and mouth. And it worked – well, sort of. Still alive three quarters of an hour later, and long after his gallows companions had ceased 'dancing the Tyburn hornpipe' he was cut down and carried to a nearby house. There Mr Chovet opened a vein or two and bled him; Gordan opened his mouth several times but only to emit groans – then died. Someone – possibly the good surgeon – declared that had he been cut down five minutes earlier, he might have recovered. Well, he would say that, wouldn't he?

Whenever a convicted criminal was reprieved, Irish hangman Tom Galvin would complain long and bitterly about anyone 'taking the bread out of the mouth of a poor old man.' He was well known for his impatience on the scaffold, cursing the victim if he paused too long on the ladder to complete his final prayers.

'Long life to you!' Galvin would exclaim exasperatedly, 'Make haste with your prayers – the people round the swing-swong is getting tired of waiting!'

Andrew Marshall

Some executioners failed to use the correct 'left over right, right over left' recipe when binding their victims' wrists together with cords; others used straps but did not tighten them sufficiently. But one Scottish executioner went one worse by not securing the felon's arms at all! When ex-soldier Andrew Marshall was found guilty on charges of robbery and murder and was given no alternative but to keep a certain appointment on the scaffold, he neglected to remind his dispatcher that he should have had his arms bound; instead, after the noose had been positioned round his neck, and before the rope started to tighten, he promptly reached up and took firm hold of the gallows' beam with both hands.

At such an unexpected move on the part of the condemned man, the hangman took the action recommended in the unwritten rules of the *Executioners' Manual*; he grabbed the man around the waist and clung to him. Tactics such as these were successful only when a felon was hanging by his neck, not when he was hanging on by his arms, so the hangman, no doubt thinking rapidly before the now-frenzied crowd rushed the scaffold, did what any self-respecting and resourceful executioner would be expected to do under those difficult circumstances; seizing a stick he proceeded to batter the victim's hands with it so violently that eventually Marshall had to release his hold – and die.

Robber John Williams, found guilty of murdering a policeman in 1912 during an attempted break-in, was sentenced to death. His girlfriend, who had recently given birth to their child, visited him in the condemned cell, taking the baby with her. When saying goodbye, Williams put a piece of prison bread into the infant's hand, curled its fingers around it, and commented, 'There you are – now nobody can say that your father never gave you anything!'

James McDonnell and Charles Sharpe

After the Civil War in America, hundreds of immigrants from Poland, Ireland, Germany and Wales poured into the Pennsylvanian mining regions and not unnaturally, in view of the differences in the languages and cultures, kept their own community spirit alive by forming small social societies, their basic aim being Christian cooperation and friendship with all. As time went by, however, an Irish group, originally named the Buckshots, was taken over by criminals. Known as the Molly Maguires, these gangsters established similar 'chapters' in other towns, spreading a reign of terror throughout the territory. Blackmail, protection rackets, even murder, became the order of the day, until eventually the mine-owners employed James McParlan, an employee of Pinkerton's, the world-famous detective agency, to infiltrate the gang's inner council and obtain evidence which would stand up in a court of law. At the risk of his life, McParlan ingratiated himself with the criminals and became an accepted member.

Some little time afterwards, on 6 July 1875, a policeman was murdered by the gang, this being followed on 3 September by the killing of a mine-owner. The latter had been slain by Michael Boyle and Edward Kelly, their accomplice being James Kerrigan whose testimony, together with that obtained by the Pinkerton detective, resulted in others of the gang being rounded up. Charles Sharpe and James McDonnell were among those who were charged and found guilty of committing other murders across the region, including the murder of a coal operator, George K. Smith. The *New York World* regaled its readers with its version of the proceedings:

'Charles Sharpe and James McDonnell slept well last night and Sharpe was enjoying the soundest kind of midnight nap when the turnkey went to McDonnell's cell at that hour to rouse him for prayers, as he had requested. This morning however they failed to eat any breakfast, probably on account of the religious services in McDonnell's cell. Sharpe's wife, child, brother and a number of other relatives, and McDonnell's three brothers were present.

A telegram from Pottsville worried those in charge of the

execution. It announced that Mrs McDonnell and her children were on their way to say goodbye to their husband and father. After a consultation it was agreed that the meeting might unnerve McDonnell and it was thought best not to wait for the arrival of the family, whose train would not get in until after 10.30, the hour agreed on with the priests for the execution.

At 10.26, just when the crowd was beginning to show signs of impatience, the sheriff knocked at the doors of the men's cells. Ten minutes later the men appeared and the procession marched the short distance to the scaffold. The doomed men walked erect, with a firm tread, and seemed to have no trouble in ascending the ten high steps to the scaffold. A short service was at once begun and in their responses the prisoners exhibited a firmness of tone that was lacking in the priests.

When the service ended the sheriff said, 'James McDonnell, have you anything to say before I proceed further?' McDonnell replied in a low voice as if a little embarrassed at speaking before so large an audience, 'Me and Sharpe have been together often. He is innocent of killing Smith. I am innocent of any murder except the one I confessed' (that of a man named Patrick Burns).

The sheriff turned to Sharpe and asked him if he had anything to say. Sharpe replied in a firm voice, 'I declare I am as innocent of the murder of George K. Smith as a child unborn.' Turning to McDonnell he then said with emphasis, 'James McDonnell, you are innocent of the Smith murder.' He whispered a few words to Father Bunce and then said, 'I desire to return my thanks to the sheriff and his family and the turnkey,' and McDonnell blurted out, 'I the same.' Then McDonnell looked toward one of his brothers who was standing at the foot of the scaffold and said abruptly, 'Give that man five dollars,' but no one knew what he meant, and his dying legacy will probably never be paid.

The arms and the legs of the criminals were pinioned and the priests left the gallows. The sheriff and his assistants soon followed, the sheriff taking with him the rope attached to the drop, and waited a few moments for Father Bunce to give the signal by dropping his handkerchief. However, just as the sheriff descended from the scaffold, a telegraph boy with a reprieve rang the jail's front door bell, but neither the prisoners nor the executioner heard or heeded the sound. Father Bunce's handkerchief dropped, the sheriff pulled the rope, and Sharpe and McDonnell fell with a heavy thud. Their bodies twirled until the twist was out of the rope; Sharpe struggled violently for a minute and then both men hung as limp as wet rags.

All at once there was a commotion and the word 'reprieve' was on everybody's lips. The news of the receipt of the dispatch nearly crazed the brothers of Sharpe and McDonnell, who had stood almost unconcernedly throughout the whole proceedings, the nearest men to the scaffold. They called the sheriff a murderer and denounced the authorities generally, but Father Bunce took the poor men aside and explained the matter to them, and they then became quieter. The good father explained that the executions had to go ahead when they did because the timing had been agreed on by himself and the sheriff with the consent of the prisoners.

In the excitement the bodies had been completely forgotten and were not cut down for thirty minutes. Sharpe's heart ceased to beat eight minutes after the drop fell, but McDonnell's neck had been broken and he was thirteen minutes in dying. Friends took possession of the remains and they were taken to their former homes by the first train.'

And the reprieve? Well, that had been granted by the State Governor on a minor legal point which was decided later that day, and the men would have been hanged on the following Monday anyway.

In 1761 Isaac Darking, a notorious highwayman, was caught and sentenced to death. Nonchalant to the last, he spent his last night drinking in the condemned cell and reading The Beggars' Opera. *Next morning on the scaffold he blithely waved the hangman away and casually positioned the noose around his own neck.*

John M'Naughton

A dashing and debonair Irishman, M'Naughton proved attractive to most women, but the young lady he had set his sights on was the teenaged daughter of Richard Knox, a local landowner, and he redoubled his efforts on discovering that her dowry would amount to no less than £15,000. Accordingly he consistently declared the depth of his affections for her and, eventually finding her alone in her parents' house one day, he produced a prayer book and read out the marriage service to her. It would seem that Miss Knox, although so overwhelmed by this handsome and much sought after man's declaration of devotion for her that she gave the correct answers, was nevertheless cautious enough to add after each reply the proviso 'provided my father consents.'

M'Naughton took no notice of the verbal codicil and proudly boasted of his married state to all and sundry. However, on then being warned by her father not to see her again, his mood changed to one of defiance and he repeated his claim in the local newspapers. The Knoxes retaliated by issuing a statement on oath, describing in detail the mock ceremony which had taken place in their house. On realising that the dowry was now beyond his reach and insensate with vengeful rage M'Naughton lay in wait for Miss Knox's coach and, forcing the coachman to rein in the horses, flung open the door and fired five shots from his pistol, killing her outright.

Arrested and put on trial at Lifford, he claimed that his intention was not to harm her but simply to take her home as his lawfully wedded wife; moreover he produced in evidence a letter purportedly written by her, in which she declared her longing to be with him. His fate was sealed, however, when the letter was proved to be a forgery.

Despite the murder he had committed, the public had fallen

victim to his daredevil charisma and found excuses for him, the general opinion being that he had been driven to it by being thwarted of winning the woman he loved; indeed, so inclined were they in his favour that the authorities found it impossible to find carpenters willing to construct a scaffold, and the girl's family had to set to and make one themselves – though doubtless they took a certain amount of vengeful satisfaction in so doing. The carpenters were not the only ones declining to cooperate; before M'Naughton was led out to the scaffold it was necessary to have his leg-irons removed, however, the local blacksmith refused to do so until compelled by soldiers who had been summoned by the Sheriff.

The execution took place at Strabane on 13 December 1762. M'Naughton lived up to his reputation; smartly dressed, wearing a white waistcoat, he bowed to the immense crowd before the cap covered his face and the noose settled around his neck, a gesture the onlookers no doubt appreciated. But his moment of truth had arrived: he might have charmed women; he might have mesmerised the general public, but it was the hangman he really fell for! However, that official let him down – although not until he had hanged him twice, for without warning the condemned man suddenly leapt from the scaffold, snapping the rope, and so had to be brought back to wait until a new one was procured and its ends attached, one round the beam, the other encircling M'Naughton's neck, death coming none too quickly.

An assassination attempt on 28 July 1835 by Corsican Marco Fieschi failed to kill King Louis-Philippe but caused death and injury among the crowd, the more so because the weapon employed consisted of nearly fifty rifles mounted in a wooden frame, all set to fire simultaneously. On leaving for the guillotine the executioner, noticing that the would-be assassin

wore only vest and pants, offered him a coat. Cynical to the last, Fieschi replied, 'Don't waste your time – I'll be a lot colder when they bury me!'

Mohammed Ali

Scaffolds are usually made large enough to accommodate not only the victim and executioner, but also officials such as the chaplain, prison governor, sheriff and surgeon, but this was definitely not the case at one particular execution in India, as related by Robert Elliot in *The Experiences of a Planter in the Jungles of Mysore*, published in 1871. He wrote:

'The criminal, Mohammed Ali, after his fetters had been removed, was handed his breakfast, which, strange as it may seem, he slowly consumed in the presence of some five hundred onlookers, and within sight of the tree with its dangling rope, and the newly dug grave for the reception of his corpse.

Having eaten and drunk his fill, he took leave of his wife and relatives, and mounted the six-foot-high narrow platform directly under the rope. His hands and feet were pinioned, a bag fixed over his head, and the noose coiled in readiness. But the rope was then found to be too short; it was ordered to be lengthened, and in the confusion that ensued, the policemen who were supporting the victim both commenced to fumble at the rope. The bench on which they stood was not eighteen inches wide and the consequence was that, in a second, the prisoner, unable to see, lost his balance and fell off, with stunning force, on to his face. He uttered no cry, but groaned heavily two or three times. As they raised him off the ground, apparently half insensible, I shall never forget the impression made upon me by the sight of the limply dangling limbs, and the blood which, streaming down his face, stained crimson the white cotton cloth with which his head was enveloped.

The rope had now been lengthened, and the unhappy man was half-lifted, half-supported on to the bench, and he died without a struggle. I turned immediately to scan the countenances of the people, in order to gather, if possible, the impression the scene had made on them, and as I looked at man after man, and expression after expression, I felt convinced that these, at any rate, were not the apathetic Asiatics I had read of, and that, on the whole, they felt much as I did.'

Sergeant Raoulx was one of the 'Four Sergeants of La Rochelle' who were condemned to death for plotting mutiny against the French royal family. On 21 September 1822 the executioners Henri Sanson and his son went to the prison for the routine preparation of their prisoners. Resigned but still spirited, they submitted to having their hair cut short; Raoulx was the most cheerful, alluding to his own lack of inches, he joked, 'Poor me – how much will remain of me when my head is gone?'

James Murphy

Probably the most important piece of the hangman's equipment was the rope. Of course it had to be strong; nineteenth-century English executioners generally used ropes made of Italian hemp, about three quarters of an inch thick, consisting of five strands, each of one-ton breaking strain. It also had to be pliable, so that the noose would tighten quickly, thin enough to run through the noose easily, but not thin enough to act like a cheesewire and decapitate the victim. It is to be regretted therefore that the American hangman who dispatched murderer James Murphy in 1876 did not follow the English example.

The execution took place in Ohio, and after the felon had been allowed to voice the almost traditional warnings to the audience against the inherent dangers of drink and sinful living, the hangman operated the drop. And the rope promptly snapped above Murphy's head. He fell through the gaping hole beneath his feet and collapsed on the ground below in a huddled heap, where he was heard to moan, 'My God, I ain't dead!'

Warders rushed to his assistance and he was helped to his feet, being comforted by the priest while others hastily attached a new, thicker rope to the gallows' beam. Then the limp, choking victim was supported up the steps, back on to the scaffold, there to be repositioned on the trapdoors where, with a warder on each side holding him upright at arm's length lest they too accompanied him into the pit, the drop was operated – and this time the rope held.

Notorious murderer Charles Peace was condemned to be hanged on 25 February 1879. Eating his last breakfast, he exclaimed, 'This is bloody rotten bacon!'

Later, in the lavatory, he shouted to an impatient warder, 'You're in a hell of a hurry – who's going to be hanged, me or you?'

Native Americans

During the American Civil War, Native Americans took advantage of the government's preoccupation with hostilities to attack the white farming families who lived along the Minnesota border. Large numbers of braves, led by Little Crow, brutally killed more than 490 settlers, nor did they spare the women and children. A strong force of soldiers under the command of General John Pope met and defeated the warrior force, 308 of the survivors being captured and sentenced to death by military court. President Lincoln, however, ruled that only the most savage of the killers, 38 in number, should be hanged. Their executions were scheduled to take place simultaneously, on 26 December 1862, at Mankato, Minnesota.

The preparations were organised with military precision; four days earlier an order was read out for the benefit of everyone living in that township and the adjoining territory for a distance of ten miles from the headquarters, requiring them not to sell

173

or give any intoxicating liquors to the enlisted men of the United States' forces.

Meanwhile the 38 condemned Native Americans had been moved into a separate apartment away from their comrades, and were visited by the colonel and others, the officer reading out to them the President's approval of their sentences and the order confirming their execution, the statement being translated into the Dakota language. It read:

'Your Great Father in Washington, after carefully reading what the witnesses have testified in your several trials, has come to the conclusion that you have each been guilty of wantonly and wickedly murdering his white children; and for this reason he has directed that you each be hanged by the neck until you are dead, on next Friday, and the order will be carried into effect on that day at ten o'clock in the forenoon.'

The *St Paul Pioneer* reported:

'the Indians listened attentively and at the end of each sentence, gave their usual grunt or signal of approval.

On the Tuesday evening they extemporised a dance with a wild Indian song. It was feared that this was only a cover for something else which might be attempted, and the chains which tied them in pairs were fastened to the floor. It seems, however, rather probable that they were singing their death song. Their friends from the other prison had been in to bid them farewell and they were now ready to die. On Thursday the women employed as cooks for the prisoners were admitted to the prison. Locks of hair, blankets, coats and almost every other article in the possession of the prisoners were given in trust for some relative or friend.

On the Friday the Revd Father Ravoux visited the condemned men, finding that little conversation passed between them, though occasionally one would mutter a few words to another in an unintelligible jargon. Most of them lay on the floor in as comfortable a position as their chains would allow, unconcernedly smoking their pipes as if they were engaged in council over some unimportant matter of tribal concern and their lives were not destined to end in three or four short hours' time.

While the padre was speaking to them, one, Old Tazoo, broke out into a death wail, in which one after the other joined in, until the prison room was filled with a wild, unearthly plaint which was neither of grief or despair, but rather a paroxysm of savage passion. During the lulls in their death-song they would resume their pipes and, with the exception of an occasional mutter or the rattling of their chains, they sat motionless and impassive until one among the elder would break out in the wild wail, when all would join in again, in the solemn preparation for death.'

Following this, the Revd Dr Williamson addressed them in their native tongue, after which they broke out again into their song of death. This was described as:

'thrilling beyond belief of expression; the trembling voices, their forms shaking with passionate emotion, the half-uttered words through set teeth, all made up a scene which no one who saw it can ever forget. The influence of the wild music of their death-song was almost magical, their whole manner changing after they had closed their singing, and an air of cheerful unconcern marked all of them. As their friends came about them they bade them cheerful farewell and in some cases there would be peals of laughter as they were wished pleasant journeys to the spirit world. They bestowed their pipes upon their favourites and so far as they had any, gave keepsakes to all.

They had evidently taken great pains to make themselves presentable for their last appearance on the stage of life. Most of them had little pocket mirrors, and before they were bound, employed themselves in putting on the finishing touches of paint and arranging their hair according to the Indian mode. Many were painted in war style, with bands and beads and feathers, and were decked as gaily as for a festival.

As those at the head of the procession came out of the basement, we heard a sort of death-wail sounded, which was immediately caught up by all the condemned and was chanted in unison until the foot of the scaffold was reached. At the foot of the steps there was no delay. Captain Redfield mounted the drop, at the head, and the Indians crowded after him as if it were a race to see who would get up first. They actually crowded on each other's heels and as they got to the top, they took up their positions, forming long rows, without any assistance from those detailed for that purpose. They still kept up a mournful wail and occasionally there would be a piercing scream.

The ropes were soon arranged around their necks, not the least resistance being offered. One or two, feeling the noose uncomfortably tight, attempted to loosen it, and although their hands were tied, they partially succeeded. The movement, however, was noticed by the assistants, and the cords rearranged. The white caps, which had been placed on the top of their heads, were now drawn down over their faces, shutting out forever the light of day from their eyes.

Then ensued a scene that can hardly be described and which can never be forgotten. All joined in shouting and singing, as it appeared to those who were ignorant of the language. The tones seemed somewhat discordant and yet there was harmony to it. Their bodies swayed to and fro and their every limb seemed to be keeping time. The drop trembled and shook as if all were dancing. The most touching scene on the drop were their attempts to grasp each other's hands, fettered as they were. They were very close to each other and many succeeded. Three or four in a row were hand in hand, swaying up and down with the rise and fall of their voices. One old man reached out each side but could not grasp a hand; his struggles were piteous and affected many onlookers. We were informed by those who understood the language that their singing and dancing was only to sustain each other, that there was nothing defiant in their last moments, and that no death-song, strictly speaking, was ever chanted on the gallows. Each one shouted his own name and called the name of his friend, saying in substance, 'I'm here! I'm here!'

The traps were held in place by wooden posts placed upright beneath them, and at one tap of the drum, almost drowned by the voices of the Indians, first one, then another of the stays were knocked away by the soldiers, and with a crash, down came the drops. All the Indians were instantly jerked downwards by their own weight; however the rope by which one was suspended broke, and his body came down on the boards with a heavy crash and a thud. There was no struggling by any of the Indians for the space of half a minute; the only movements were the natural vibrations caused by the fall. In the meantime a new rope was placed round the neck of the one who had fallen and, it having been thrown over the beam, he was soon hanging with the others. After the lapse of a minute, several drew up their legs once or twice, and there was some movement of their arms. One Indian, at the expiration of ten minutes, still breathed, but the rope was better adjusted and life was soon extinct.

The bodies were left hanging for about half an hour, the physicians then reporting that life was extinct. Soon after, several United States' mule teams appeared and the bodies were taken down and dumped into the wagons without much ceremony. They were transported down to the sandbar in front of the city and all buried in the same hole. Everything was conducted in the most orderly and quiet manner. As the wagons bore the bodies of the murderers off to burial, the people quietly dispersed.'

The journalist concluded by saying, 'It is unnecessary to speak of the awful sight of 38 human beings being suspended in the air. Imagination will readily supply what we refrain from describing.'

177

It is unlikely that such a horrific scene will ever occur again; as far as is known, it was the greatest number of victims ever to be hanged at the same time.

A ruthless and cold-blooded murderer, John Thurtell was tried and condemned to death in 1824, a penalty which left him so unmoved that on hearing directions being given by a surgeon to the students who would be dissecting him after his execution, he listened unconcernedly and took a pinch of snuff. In the condemned cell he expressed much interest in the possible outcome of a bout of fisticuffs shortly to take place between two famous pugilists, Tom Spring and Langan, at Worcester racecourse. At dawn on the day following the bout, Thurtell, the gallows looming up before him, spoke his last words. 'Who won the big fight, I wonder?' he asked.

Elizabeth and Josiah Potts

Too long a drop decapitated, too short a drop strangled; although the former must have been the more horrendous spectacle for witnesses, it probably brought a quicker, more merciful death to the victim, and in 1890 in Nevada a story of both errors unfolded, the victims being Josiah Potts and his wife Elizabeth.

They had both been found guilty of murder; on the scaffold they embraced and declared their love for each other before the sheriff operated the drop, sending both plunging into the waiting pit. It was then that disaster struck. The noose tightened around Josiah's throat, death taking seemingly aeons of time; it was reported that he lived for a further fifteen minutes. However, Elizabeth was a large lady and while the length of drop brought a slow death to her husband, her weight imposed such a strain on a rope of the same length that the noose severed her windpipe, an artery and the fleshy parts of her throat, blood thereby gushing copiously over her clothes. But she did at least suffer for a shorter time than did her husband.

American Arthur Gooch, a habitual criminal, broke out of jail and in an ensuing gun battle, shot and injured a police officer. He was captured, tried and sentenced to death. Due to be hanged at midnight on 19 June 1936, he had previously persuaded the prison warden to obtain a radio for him so that he could listen to the world heavyweight championship fight between Joe Louis and Max Schmeling, scheduled for that evening, a Thursday. However, the fight was postponed for twenty-four hours, Gooch commenting dryly, 'Won't need a radio if it's going to be Friday night – I'll be up there somewhere; think I'll float over and grab myself a seat right above the ring!'

Dr William Pritchard

William Calcraft

The hangman William Calcraft was essentially a family man; he bred rabbits, kept a pony, grew flowers and loved fishing. He had only one failing: he rarely, if ever, gave his client a drop of more than three feet, if that; consequently most of them were throttled to death. At that time, such a method was standard practice; no one ever considered that there could be, or should be, a more humane alternative; the criminal deserved their punishment, and anyway, a speedy, merciful method of hanging would reduce entertainment time for the good folk clustered round the scaffold to a mere minute or two – and that would never do! One who stayed suspended on the end of Calcraft's rope for an unconscionable length of time was Dr William Pritchard.

A medical practitioner in Glasgow, Dr Pritchard was somewhat of a fantasist, constantly boasting of his close friendship with foreign statesmen whom he had never met and giving lectures about countries he had never visited. Such mild eccentricities could easily be overlooked by Victorian society; what could definitely not be ignored were the suspicious deaths, first of his mother-in-law, Mrs Jane Taylor, and later of his wife, Mary Jane (Minnie), whom he had married fifteen years earlier. Regrettably, suspicions initiated by an anonymous letter were confirmed, post-mortems revealing that they had both been poisoned by eating some tapioca pudding which contained opium, antimony and aconite.

At his trial for murder in 1865 the accused man tried to blame one of the housemaids, a young girl named Mary M'Leod whom, he averred, had been his mistress (she had earlier become pregnant by him and he had employed his medical skills in carrying out an abortion), and he accused her of murdering his wife so that he could marry her. The maid, while agreeing that she had been his mistress, tearfully declared that he had indeed promised to marry her if his wife should die, but that she had played no part in the crimes. Even if she had, her defence pointed out, why should she have also killed her employer's mother-in-law? And when the jury heard a local chemist testify that the prisoner had frequently purchased antimony from his pharmacy, and that Mrs Pritchard would inherit a large sum of money in the event of her mother's death, the fact that the older lady had died first left them in no doubt as to Pritchard's culpability. They brought in a verdict of guilty, and the judge wasted little time in pronouncing the death sentence.

The date of the execution happened to coincide with the annual Glasgow Fair, a gala which always attracted a multitude of visitors, and the council had to arrange for the removal of some of the roundabouts and sideshows in order to accommodate what was definitely not a sideshow, the scaffold itself, around which, as the time drew near, more than 100,000 spectators thronged, order being maintained by some 750 police constables.

Understandably the case and the verdict produced a furore in Scotland, the newspapers of the day selling a record number of copies, all devoting page after page to the poisoner's and his family's background, their way of life and his way of death. The *Edinburgh Scotsman* gave a 'fly-on-the-wall' account of the day's proceedings:

'the prisoner retired to bed a little before midnight on his last night, and although he was somewhat restless at first he soon fell into a deep sleep and slept soundly until five o'clock in the morning. When he rose he seemed to be perfectly calm and gave his attendants the impression that he was more lively and cheerful than he had been since his removal to Glasgow. He partook of some coffee and bread that had been provided for him and

181

appeared quite prepared for the dreadful ordeal which he was to go through.

His appearance on the scaffold was the signal for a deep howl of execration from the immense crowd. Among those present were a number of modellers from Edinburgh who had received the sanction of the authorities to take a cast of the culprit's head after execution to enrich the collection of similar curiosities in the museum of the Phrenological Society. Calcraft, the executioner, stepped on to the scaffold along with the doomed man and was received with a few groans and hisses. Quietly, and with an expertness that showed him to be well accustomed to his awful work, the executioner stationed his victim above the drop and busied himself in the grim work of his office. The white cap was expeditiously drawn over the head of the culprit and the fatal noose adjusted about his neck. The prominent figure of the executioner, his head covered by a black skull cap and his long white beard lending to his aspect a sort of venerable air, strongly attracted the attention of the crowd and drew forth repeated sounds of recognition.

The dread preparations having been completed, Calcraft stepped a pace or two backward on the scaffold and anxiously surveyed the rope that was to suspend the victim. He seemed satisfied with the result of his scrutiny for he again advanced, examined the rope about the prisoner's neck, taking particular care to see that his beard was free from its influence, and then grasped the unhappy man by the hand and shook it kindly and almost affectionately in token of farewell. This token of feeling on the part of the aged executioner [he was then 65] seemed to meet with the approval of the crowd and once more the hoarse murmur spread through their ranks. Firmly the prisoner stood above the drop, showing little if any trace of agitation except an occasional quiver of the legs, and several times Calcraft, as if morbidly anxious that no mistake should occur, examined the rope and drop to see that all was clear.

After finally completing his scrutiny he pulled the bolt and the body of the prisoner swung with a sudden jerk into space. The unhappy man did not die without a struggle. For an instant after the drawing of the bolt no motion was perceptible in the body but it soon swung quickly around, the whole form quivering and the hands working with muscular action. But this soon ceased and ere ten minutes had elapsed his body hung perfectly motionless upon the rope in the dull air of the morning.'

The body remained hanging until fourteen minutes past nine, when Calcraft proceeded to lower it. In doing so, despite the 'expertness' lauded by the newspaper, he suddenly lost his grip of the rope, and the cadaver fell violently on to the coffin, which was resting on two trestles in the pit below. Part of the bottom was knocked out but was quickly repaired by a number of the fair's workmen who were present among the crowd, and the body, once stripped, was then carried back into the courthouse where, after the modellers had taken the cast of the murderer's head, the body was buried in the courtyard of the gaol.

The Gentleman's Magazine *of February 1767 reported that 'having been condemned for a street robbery at Cork, Ireland, Patrick Redmond was executed and hung by a short rope for upwards of twenty-eight minutes, when the mob, led by his colleague and fellow robber Glover, carried off the body to a place previously appointed, where he was, after five or six hours, actually recovered by a surgeon, who made the incision in his throat called bronchotomy, which produced the desired effect. The poor fellow has just received his pardon, and it is recorded that he had the hardihood to go to the local theatre the same evening. There he mounted the stage to tumultuous applause and gave full credit to his friend – whereupon the audience took up a genteel collection for him.'*

Will Purvis

One would never have thought that escaping the gallows would be a snip, least of all Will Purvis – but it was! It all started back in 1893 in Columbia, Mississippi, when gangs known as the White Caps, successors to the first incarnation of the infamous Ku Klux Klan, terrorised the local black population. One of their victims, a servant of one of the organisation's members, Will Bradley, was seized and severely flogged without his employer being aware of it. Outraged at this taking place without his knowledge, Bradley shopped his colleagues, reporting them to the authorities, as a result of which three of those responsible were taken into custody. On his way home after giving evidence, Bradley, his brother Jim, and the servant involved were ambushed; Bradley was shot and killed outright but the other two managed to escape.

It so happened that the attack took place near the home of the Purvis family and one of their neighbours, having a grudge against them, aroused the locals against 19-year-old Will Purvis to such an extent that he was arrested and put in jail, charged with being one of Bradley's attackers. Despite friends providing an alibi for him and testifying that he had been nowhere near the scene of the shooting on the night in question, Will Bradley's brother Jim swore that he recognised the accused as one of the attackers. At that the jury found Will Purvis guilty and he was sentenced to be hanged.

The *New Orleans Item* newspaper, in an article written over two decades later in 1920, rolled back the intervening years and gave what purported to be a melodramatic eyewitness account of what happened on the scaffold on that day, 7 February 1894.

'With face bleached by confinement within prison walls but with firm and steady eye young Purvis ascends the scaffold. As he looks over that closely packed and vacuously yawping throng the young man sees few friendly faces. Feeling against him has been intense and most people believe he is about to expiate a crime for which he should pay the extreme penalty. Everyone is waiting for one thing before the final drop. It is the confession of the boy that he did commit murder. But Purvis speaks simply these plain words which amaze them, 'You are taking the life of an innocent man. There are people here who know who did commit the crime and if they will come forward and confess I will go free.'

As Purvis finishes his simple plea the sheriff and three deputies adjust the rope around his neck, his feet and arms are pinioned, and the black cap is placed over his face. All is ready, but the meticulous deputy sees an ungainly rope's end sticking out. One must be neat at such functions and he steps up and snips the end flush with the knot.

'Tell me when you are ready,' Purvis remarks, not knowing that the doomed man is never given this information lest he brace himself.

Nothing is heard save the persistent and importunate praying of the minister. The executioner takes the hatchet. As he draws it back to sever the stay rope holding the trap on which Purvis stands, strong men tremble and a woman screams and faints. The blow descends, the trap falls, and the body of Purvis darts like a plummet downward towards the sharp jerk of a sudden death.

Terror and awe gripped the throng as Purvis fell towards his death. Those few men who had watched other hangings have averted their faces. Others who had never witnessed a like event and who could not appreciate the morbid horror of it, stared open-mouthed. But those who looked did not see the boy dangle and jerk and become motionless in death. The rope failed to perform the service ordained for it by law. Instead of tightening like a garrotter's bony finger on the neck of the youth, the hangman's knot untwisted and Purvis fell to the ground unhurt, save for a few abrasions on his skin caused by the slipping of the rope.

185

No tongue can describe and no pen can indite the feeling of horror that seized and held the vast throng. For a moment the watchers remained motionless; then moved by an impelling wonder, they crowded forward, crushing one another with the force of their movement. In a moment the silence broke. Excited murmurs began to emanate from the crowd. 'What's the matter? Did the noose slip?' someone asked. Others wondered if there had been some trick in tying the knot. But those charged with the duty of making it fast said there was not, and their statement was verified by a committee that had examined the rope and the knot just before its adjustment around the man's neck.

Somewhat dazed, Purvis staggered to his feet. The black cap had slipped from his face and the large blue eyes of the boy blinked in the sunlight. Most of the crowd stood dumfounded [sic] and the officials were aghast. Purvis realised the situation sooner than any of them and turning to the sheriff, said, 'Let's have it over with.' At the same time the boy, bound hand and foot as he was, began to hop towards the steps of the scaffold, and had mounted the first step before the silence was broken.

An uneasy tremor swept the crowd. The slight cleavage in the opinion which before had been manifest concerning the boy's guilt or innocence now seemed to widen into a real division. Many of those who had been most urgent that Purvis be hanged, began to feel within themselves the first flutter of misgiving. This feeling might never have been crystallised into words had it not been for a simple little incident. One of the officials on the platform reached for the end of the rope [hanging down into the pit] but found that it was just beyond his fingers' ends. Stooping, he called out to Dr Ford, who was standing beneath, 'Toss that rope up here, will you, Doctor?' Dr Ford started mechanically to obey. He picked up the rope and looked at it. The crowd watched him intently. Here was a man who had been most bitter against the White Caps, a man who knew that Purvis had been a member of that notorious body, and yet everyone knew that he was one of the few who refused to believe the boy was guilty. Throwing the rope down, he said, "I won't do any such damn thing. That boy's been hung once too many times now."

Electrically the crowd broke its silence. Cries of 'Don't let him hang!' were heard clashing with 'Hang him! He's guilty!' A few of Purvis' friends and relatives were galvanised into action. They pushed their way forward, ready to act, but the greater proportion of the spectators were still morbidly curious to see the death struggles of the boy. Some of them really believed the ends of justice were about to be thwarted, and tensed themselves to prevent any attempt to free him.

At that moment the Revd J. Sibley, whose sympathy and prayer had helped to sustain the mother during her trying ordeal, sprang up the steps of the scaffold ahead of the stumbling boy. He was a preacher of the most eloquent type and of fine physique and commanding appearance. His eyes flashed with the fire of a great inspiration as he raised his hands and stood motionless until the eyes of the spectators became centred on him. 'All who want to see this boy hanged a second time,' he shouted, 'hold up their hands.'

The crowd remained transfixed. There is a difference between the half-shamed desire of a man to stand in a large throng and watch his neighbour die, and the willingness of that man to stand before others and signify by raising his hand that he insisted upon the other's extinction. Not a hand went up. 'All who are opposed to hanging Will Purvis a second time,' cried the Reverend Sibley, 'hold up your hands.' Every hand in the crowd went up as if magically raised by a universal lever.

Pandemonium ensued. Men tore their hair and threw their hats into the air, swearing that this man should not be hanged again. Public sentiment had changed in an instant. Before the hanging they thought him a vile and contemptible murderer, now they believed him spotless as an angel.

The sheriff and his deputies were undoubtedly in an awkward position. They had been commissioned to carry out the sentence of the court and they were bound by their oaths of office to do so. Should they flout the authority of the court merely because a number of emotional spectators had decided out of hand not to allow the defendant to be hanged, they would be liable to impeachment and imprisonment. On the other hand, to attempt to hang Purvis a second time in the face of 5,000 healthy spectators, nearly every one determined to prevent such action, would be suicide.

Dr Ford suggested that a judge or lawyer be sought. Finally a young attorney answered the summons. After considering the matter in its various aspects, he reluctantly informed the sheriff that it was his belief that Purvis must be 'hanged by the neck until dead' according to the meaning of the sentence. The sheriff just as reluctantly agreed.

Dr Ford, who had listened with chagrin to the attorney's opinion, finally spoke up with determination. 'I don't agree with you. Now, if I go up on the scaffold and ask three hundred men to stand by me and prevent the hanging, what are you going to do about it?'

Both the sheriff and the attorney were taken aback at this suggestion. They realised that they would be powerless in the face of such action. 'I'm ready to do it too,' added Dr Ford. Suddenly the sheriff turned, walked to Purvis and, as the crowd cheered, began to loosen the bonds of the prisoner. It was with difficulty that Purvis was carried back to jail, so persistent was the crowd in its demand for his freedom.

Henry Banks, one of the staff of executioners, afterwards gave his version as to why the knot had slipped. 'The rope was too thick in the first place,' he said. 'It was made of new grass and was very springy. After the first man tied the noose, he left the free end hanging out. It was this way when the tests were made, but when it came to placing this knot around Purvis' neck, it looked untidy. The hangman didn't want to be accredited with this kind of job, so he cut the rope flush with the noose knot. It looked neat, but when the weight of Purvis was thrown against it, the rope slipped and the knot became untied.'

There the newspaper article ended, but why was it not written until 1920? Well, Purvis was indeed returned to his cell and the legal wrangling commenced. The American Constitution makes double jeopardy (being tried twice for the same offence) illegal, but the Mississippi Supreme Court rejected that ruling on the grounds that Purvis was not being tried twice, but hanged twice, and so decreed that he should mount the scaffold again. But while he was awaiting execution, friends broke into the jail and helped him to escape, he then avoided capture by taking refuge in a remote part of the country.

Two years went by, and then a revelation came out of the blue; Jim Bradley, the man who had been responsible for the arrest and conviction of Will Purvis, now came forward to admit that he had doubts about his original accusation, in which he had identified Purvis as his brother's killer. But freedom was just as far as ever from the outlawed man, for the state governor, instead of pardoning Purvis, commuted his death sentence to one of life imprisonment. Obviously weary of being a wanted man, Purvis gave himself up and was returned to jail, but not for long, for on 19 December 1898, four years after his narrow escape from death, he was granted a full pardon.

But the story didn't end there. A happy ending was in the offing, although it took nineteen years to come about, for a man named Joe Beard 'got religion', responded to the fervent appeals of the Holy Rollers, an itinerant Christian organisation, and cleansed his soul by confessing all his sins, one of which was that he, together with one Louis Thornhill, murdered Will Bradley. The Legislature of Mississippi then compensated Will Purvis by awarding him the princely sum of $5,000, and the *New Orleans Item* of 6 June 1920 published their version of that long-gone execution day. But had a certain methodically minded deputy sheriff not snipped the untidy-looking end of the rope protruding from the hangman's knot . . .

The choice of the tree on which they were to be hanged was traditionally left to the condemned felon, and Scotsman Jock Donald accordingly selected a small sapling. When the sheriff pointed out that it was much too small, Donald replied, 'Och, but I'm in no hurry; I'll just wait till it grows!'

Thomas Reynolds

Two robbers, Thomas Reynolds and James Bayley, were arrested in April 1736 for going armed and disguised in order to carry out street robberies. Both were sentenced to death but Bayley was later reprieved. Reynolds joined the executioner on the Tyburn scaffold on 26 July of that year. The hangman was John Thrift, the well-meaning but highly emotional executioner who shed tears when faced with having to use the axe. This time, however, it was the rope, and it was Thomas Reynolds who was also highly strung; following which, Thrift cut his body down.

Whether the hangman, who had only been in the job for a year, was not concentrating when he positioned the noose, or if he just lost track of the time and failed to let the cadaver remain suspended for the regulation hour, will never be known; suffice it to say that when the undertaker's men started to fasten the coffin lid down, they were somewhat taken aback when the corpse suddenly sat up! Thrift, knowing his duty, and fearing the wrath of the sheriff, seized him, with every intention of hanging him again, but the mob was having none of it; rushing the scaffold they attempted to attack poor Thrift, thereby diverting the attention of the constables on duty, while others spirited Reynolds away to a safe house nearby. There he vomited three pints of blood, and his rescuers, thinking that was a sign that he was recovering, promptly gave him a glass of wine. He died.

In the days when surgeons had to rely on corpses bought from bodysnatchers to use as instructional specimens, a Professor Junkur of Halle University, Germany, had purchased two cadavers and, it being late at night, had stored them, still in the sacks in which they had been delivered, in a room adjoining his bedroom. During the night he was disturbed by strange noises and, somewhat apprehensively, went to investigate to find one sack still filled, the other torn and empty! Then he started as, in the corner of the room, he saw a ghostly pale and trembling figure of a naked man, who explained that he had been hanged but cut down while still alive; he had fainted, but on later reviving, found himself in the sack, which he had managed to tear open a moment ago. He went on to beg the professor not to report him to the authorities, because they would promptly hang him again, thoroughly this time, so Junker gave him some clothes and food, and assisted him to escape across the border into Holland. Twelve years later the professor was visiting Amsterdam when a well-dressed gentleman approached him and, calling him by name, explained that he was the 'hanged man' whose life the professor had saved, and that he was now a successful businessman, married with two bonny children. A rare happy ending to a hangman's blunder!

Joseph Samuels

England had Half-Hanged Lee and Half-Hanged Smith; Australia, not to be outdone, had Half-Hanged Samuels. And just as many English hangmen were known colloquially as 'Jack Ketch', so in nineteenth-century Australia their scaffold counterparts were called Blackbeard. Always heavily disguised, they wore a large false black beard, bushy black eyebrows, doubtless home-grown, and were always clad in wide-brimmed black hats, knee-high boots and thick leather gloves. And it was a man of suchlike terrifying appearance who accompanied Joseph Samuels on to the Sydney scaffold one day in the 1800s.

Whether completely intimidated or resigned to his fate,

Samuels allowed himself to be positioned on the drop and stood meekly as Blackbeard capped and noosed him. The hangman pulled the lever, the rope tightened – then broke. Samuels fell into the pit, from where he was not too gently collected by Blackbeard and his cohorts, and returned to the drop to be re-noosed. Again the lever was operated – but this time the rope snapped at the overhead beam.

The condemned man plunged downwards again, to lie dazed and bruised from yet another impact with the floor of the pit, only to feel himself lifted and half-carried back on to the scaffold. By this time the spectators were making their presence felt in no uncertain and decidedly Australian terms, the crescendo of abuse increasing as for the third time Blackbeard noosed his victim; and for the third time the rope gave way, this time breaking near Samuel's neck. At that, officialdom had had enough. The governor was sent for and, in view of the catastrophic circumstances, issued an immediate reprieve.

Many Sydney residents were convinced that the breaking of the rope was due either to Samuel's innocence or to Divine Intervention, but those in the know were only too aware that Blackbeard stored his ropes in a leaky shed – and it had been a very rainy winter!

It was a Tyburn tradition that 'if, en route to execution, a strumpet should beg to have the condemned man as a husband, he would be reprieved and would then marry her, so that both sinful lives would be cleansed by such a holy act.' But one felon, about to have the rope placed around his neck, happened to catch the lascivious eye of a particularly unattractive woman in the crowd; turning to the hangman he exclaimed, 'Dispatch me quickly, before I am begged!'

John Smith

They should have called him 'Lucky' Smith for despite being a habitual criminal, he certainly lived a charmed life. In actual fact he was nicknamed Half-Hanged Smith because of a last minute reprieve on the scaffold, although it certainly failed to make him mend his ways thereafter.

Unfortunately, Luttrell, the annalist and bibliographer (1637–1732), did not record the reason for Smith's reprieve, though he did describe what happened that day, 12 December 1705: 'One John Smith, condemned lately at the Old Bailey for burglary, was carried to Tyburn to be executed, and was accordingly hanged up, and after he had hung about 7 minutes, a reprieve came, so he was cut down, and immediately let blood and put into a warm bed, which, with other applications, brought him to himself with much ado.'

Another account continued:

'When he had perfectly recovered his senses he was asked what were his feelings at the time of his execution, to which he repeatedly replied in substance, that when he was turned off, he, for some time, was sensible of very great pain, occasioned by the weight of his body, and felt his spirits in a strange commotion, violently pressing upwards; that having forced their way to his head, he, as it were, saw a great blaze or glaring light which seemed to go out at his eyes with a flash, and then he lost all sense of pain. That after he was cut down and begun to come to himself, the blood and spirits forcing themselves into their former channels, put him, by a sort of pricking or shooting, to such intolerable pain, that he could have wished those hanged, who had cut him down.'

Smith not only forsook his earlier lawless career, but proceeded to denounce to the authorities criminals with whom he had been formerly acquainted. Records in respect of March 1706 show that:

'Smith, who, sometime since was half-hanged and cut down, has accused about 350 pickpockets and housebreakers who got to be [became] soldiers in the guards, the better to hide their roguery; their regiments were then mustered [paraded] and they were drawn out and shipped off for Catalonia; and about 60 women, who he also accused of such crimes, were likewise sent away to camp there.'

Nor did Smith stop there. The poacher turned gamekeeper obviously revelled in the limelight, for on 9 November of that same year 'the officers of Her Majesty's guards yesterday drew out their companies in St James's Park and were viewed by Smith and two other fellows in masks, in order to discover [identify] felons and housebreakers; out of which two sergeants with six soldiers were seized as criminals and committed to the Marshalsea Prison.'

However, his conversion to that of a law-abiding citizen was short-lived, for Smith, although having been given an unconditional pardon, was not able to resist the call of crime. Shortly afterwards he was arrested and charged with burglary, but was acquitted on a point of law. Caught again later, he was brought to court, but fortune still smiled on him, for the prosecutor died and the charge was dropped. Little was heard of him after that; either he retired to the country, or maybe spent his ill-gotten gains on a pleasure cruise to foreign parts, for it was rumoured that he drowned at sea.s

En route from Newgate to the Tyburn gallows, the grim procession halted at St Giles for 'The Bowl', the traditional 'one for the road' drink of ale

allowed to those soon to swing from the gallows. The victim, Captain Stafford, his morale undaunted, asked the landlord for a bottle of wine, saying that he had an appointment to keep, but would however pay the landlord on the way back!

Alfred Sowrey

Just as London had its Newgate Prison and execution site, so the city of Lancaster had its Castle and Chapel Yard. The Castle, with its ramparts and battlements, its towers and Norman keep, looms threateningly over the houses of the town surrounding it, and within its mighty walls is a superb courtroom and prison. The notorious Judge Jeffries once handed down lengthy and harsh sentences there, and Catholic priests and witches were condemned to death after being incarcerated in the grim cells situated deep below ground. It was also a royal residence at various times over the centuries, King John, Edward II, John of Gaunt, Henry IV and their cavalcades gracing it with their regal presence.

Alfred Sowrey was a Preston man, and he occupied one of the Castle's condemned cells, having shot and killed his fiancée. He would not have been in such a fearsome location had his original plan worked, for following the murder he attempted to shoot himself, but succeeded only in inflicting what was said to be merely a minor head wound.

Whether it was the understandable dread of his approaching execution, or whether the wound had in fact been serious enough to unhinge his mind, Sowrey's violent behaviour became almost totally uncontrollable. Even during his trial his guards and others around him felt apprehensive because of his wild gesturing and incoherent outbursts. After being found guilty, the inevitable sentence being that of death by hanging, he was returned to prison, but once there, even the administrations of the chaplain failed to calm his outbreaks of sheer panic.

On the morning of his execution, 1 August 1887, the warders braced themselves for trouble, but even they were unprepared for Sowrey's frantic resistance when James Berry, the hangman, entered the cell and attempted to pinion him, and eventually he had to be held down while the straps were tightened around his wrists. But even being thus restrained, he continued to struggle as he was half-propelled, half-carried along the corridor which led to the Chapel Yard where the scaffold awaited. As it came into view, his reactions became even more ungovernable: screaming and shouting, he went berserk, five warders having to carry him bodily up the scaffold steps and hold him while Berry approached with the intention of securing his ankles. Unable to use his arms, Sowrey lashed out wildly with his feet, one kick making contact with Berry's shin. Ignoring the excruciating pain, the hangman desperately sought to get the noose round Sowrey's neck as the distraught man, determined at all costs to thwart the gallows, shook his head from side to side, the crescendo of noise drowning the voice of the chaplain as he prayed for Sowrey's soul. Eventually the nearly exhausted warders managed to hold the condemned man still, just long enough for Berry to position the noose; swiftly the hangman darted across the boards and pulled the lever. The trapdoors opened with a crash – and peace suddenly descended on the yard, the silence broken only by the chaplain uttering the last few words of the funeral service.

And James Berry limped away to have his injured leg attended to, a wound which would leave a scar as a painful reminder of one of the most traumatic executions he had ever had to perform.

After executing one criminal at Lancaster Castle, executioner William Calcraft was asked how it must feel to be hanged. He thought for a moment, then replied, 'Well, I have heard it said that when you are tied up and your face turned to the Castle wall, and the trap falls, you see the stones expanding and contracting violently, and a similar expansion and contraction seems to take place inside your own head and breast. Then there is a rush of fire and an earthquake, your eyeballs spring out of their sockets, the Castle shoots up in the air, and you tumble down a precipice.' An accurate assessment as near as anyone can get, coming from a man who performed the duty of hangman for no fewer than 45 years, 1829–1874!

Henry Spencer

Practice makes perfect, especially for those taking up the profession of executioner, and this was never more obvious than in the case of Henry Spencer, hanged in America in 1914 for murder. The man in charge was the local sheriff who, regrettably, was a complete amateur, never having performed such a role before, especially in front of a crowd of such magnitude. On the scaffold he managed to place the noose in what he thought was the correct position about Spencer's neck, compounding his error by then, for some unknown reason, ordering the victim to be concealed from view, not upwards, with a hood to cover his face, but downwards, with a full-length, cassock-like garment which, touching the boards, hid the man's body completely. Had the sheriff positioned the noose correctly, death would have occurred much more quickly than it actually did, and the omission of the hood would not have mattered quite so much. As it was, its absence allowed the shocked crowd to watch the slowly rotating and writhing victim, gasps of horror coming from every side of the scaffold in turn on seeing his contorted features, his protruding tongue, his eyes staring and dilated, as he

197

desperately fought for breath, ten nightmarish minutes elapsing before his body finally hung limp and lifeless.

The only thing hangman Marwood had in common with Calcraft, whom he succeeded on the scaffold in 1874, was his first name: William. During his whole career, as mentioned earlier, Calcraft persisted in using a rope which permitted the victim a drop of a mere three feet or so, death coming slowly by strangulation. In marked contrast, Marwood perfected the 'long drop', the length of rope depending on the victim's weight and other physical factors, dispatching him or her quickly by severing the spinal cord. Referring scathingly to Calcraft, he commented, 'He HANGED them – I EXECUTE them!'

James Stone

This case concerns the loss of three heads; one metaphorically, when James Stone attacked his wife, and two actual decapitations, those of Mrs Stone and finally, of the murderer himself.

It happened in Washington, USA, at a time when Stone's marriage to Alberta, whom he had wedded four years before, ran into difficulties. After several rows in 1878 Alberta left him and went to stay with her sister Lavinia, a woman whom Stone vehemently blamed for the breakdown in the marriage, accusing her of influencing his wife against him, so when Alberta left the marital home, he sought revenge. Arming himself with a razor, the open, long-bladed type used daily by men in that century, he went to his sister-in-law's house and, being unable to gain entrance, broke the door down. On coming face to face with Lavinia he promptly attacked her with the weapon, inflicting severe cuts to her throat before she managed to escape into the yard. Meanwhile Alberta, who had been in an upper room, heard the commotion and came downstairs, only to find herself the target as Stone, grasping her with one hand and pulling her head back, swept the razor across her throat so violently that her head was almost severed. Dropping the razor on to her blood-soaked corpse he ran out, pursued by neighbours, who eventually caught him and handed him over to the police.

No defence attorney in the world could have persuaded a jury to bring in a verdict other than guilty, and Stone was sentenced to death. In jail his behaviour seemed to fluctuate: at times he appeared to realise his crime and the awful fate awaiting him; at other times he behaved as if it were all a charade.

A Mrs Browne, the wife of one of his previous employers, had given evidence in court, testifying that he was of good character except, she added, that at times he had an uncontrollable temper. Now she visited him in his cell, and promised him that she would ensure he was buried next to the wife he had so brutally murdered.

On 2 April 1880 the *Washington Evening Star* cleared its front page ready for its reporter's story:

'Last night the condemned man, after prayers, lay down to sleep between 9 and 10 o'clock, but one of the lights in the rotunda was kept burning in such a direction as to show into his cell and for an hour or two he was unable to go to sleep. About midnight he dozed off and rested until the clock was striking four, when he awoke, but shortly afterwards he fell asleep again and slept until six. At 8.30 he ate his breakfast; pointing to his cup, a quart measure, he said to a visitor who asked sometime later how he had enjoyed his breakfast, 'Why, I took that full of coffee, with a whole fried chicken and potatoes and other trimmings.' After this he led off singing a hymn 'I am Going Home to Jesus Tonight,' and all the prisoners on the same tier joined in and the singing was very pathetic. They then sang 'Wash Me and I Shall be Whiter than Snow,' after which Stone spent some time in walking the floor in meditation and in reading his Bible.

199

Shortly after 11 o'clock the Revd Dr Rankin, the Revd Grinkle and the Revd Gibbons arrived at the jail and some time was spent in singing, prayer and religious conversation. To one of the officers Stone said that he then felt he preferred that the law be carried out rather than that his sentence be commuted.

The prisoner, dressed in black, walked up the steps of the scaffold with a firm tread and took a position facing north. There was a short service by the attending clergymen, and when they had bid him goodbye, the noose was adjusted, the black cap placed over his face, and at ten minutes after one o'clock the trap fell.

At the moment of the fall of the body, there was a cry of horror in the enclosure, some exclaiming, 'My God, the rope has broken!' and there was a rush to see what had occurred, but one look at the ghastly scene was enough for most, for, horrible to relate, the head was totally jerked off by the fall and the body had fallen to the earth.

For a moment the head was seen to cling to the noose and then dropped, spattering the beams with gore, and then fell, to land three or four feet from the body. Blood spurted from the neck in a stream. Some of the physicians immediately went to the body, and while the blood was spurting from the neck, they felt for the pulsations of the heart, and then stated that there was still a muscular movement for about two minutes.

Dr Crook picked up the head, the black cap having fallen off, and as he did so he noticed that the lips moved and the features appeared calm.

Among the physicians the opinion was expressed that the work had been too well done. As one explained it, the condemned man was so fat [he weighed 200 lbs. and was 5'8" tall] that the muscular tissues had become weakened, and the slipping rope, having once broken the skin, the fat accelerated its further progress until it reached and broke the spinal column. Some of those present seemed to think that this was a more humane execution than when the victim is choked to death.

Mr and Mrs Browne arranged for the remains to be placed in

a vault for a month prior to being interred in a grave beside his wife. There is an impression in the community that the bodies of persons hanged are preferred by the medical schools for dissecting purposes, and the friends of the deceased took this precaution of placing the remains in the vault so that it could not be used for that purpose [after a month in the vault, putrefaction would have set in, thereby rendering the cadaver useless as a surgical specimen].'

Found guilty of plotting against Charles II, William, Lord Russell was condemned to death. On his last night in the Tower he saw the rain through his cell window. 'A pity,' he said. 'Such rain tomorrow will spoil a good show.'

Next morning he asked how much it was customary to give the executioner. When told ten guineas he said wryly, 'A pretty thing to have to give a fee to have one's head cut off!'

Ellen Thompson

Some eternal triangles end in having one corner removed, the resultant geometric shape being converted into a straight line: that of a rope having the gallows beam at one end and the victim's neck at the other. This was certainly the case where Ellen Thompson was concerned, the other angles of the triangle being her husband Billy, and her lover John Harrison.

In 1885 the Thompsons lived on a farm in North Queensland, Australia; an incompatible couple, Billy was an unyielding though not ungenerous man, Ellen strong-willed and ruthlessly determined to achieve whatever she set out to do. So strained was their relationship, so violent their frequent quarrels, that Ellen lived in the family home while Billy occupied a small cottage about a hundred yards away, but despite their estranged circumstances Billy, mindful of the future welfare of his wife and their children, on making his will, bequeathed all his money and belongings to Ellen, a decision which was to sentence him to death.

Harvest time the following year meant increased work on the farm and the employment of casual labour, one man taken on being John Harrison, an ex-British Army soldier. Whether he and Ellen genuinely fell in love, or whether she decided to use him as a means of ridding herself of her husband but not of his wealth, was never established; suffice it to say that John, a weak-minded and easily manipulated man, became completely dominated by her.

As time went by the two lovers cunningly set the scene for the murder they had planned by casually spreading rumours regarding the instability both of Billy Thompson's business affairs and his mind, insinuating further that his desperation might even lead to suicide. Then late at night on 2 October 1886, they acted. On seeing the lights of the cottage extinguished, the two lovers crept up to the door. Ellen waited outside, John, with the loaded shotgun, entered and, pointing the weapon at the sleeping man's forehead, pulled the trigger. Then throwing the gun down on the bed, he and Ellen fled, he to his sleeping quarters, she to summon help for her husband who, she claimed, had just committed suicide.

After subsequent investigation, the local police discounted the suicide theory, it being considered difficult, if not impossible, to aim a long barrelled shotgun at one's own forehead, then pull the trigger. Nor had the deceased used one of his toes to fire the gun, for the blankets were still drawn up over his body. And following reports of the couple's intimate relationship, they were charged with murder.

The trial took place in May 1887 in the Supreme Court at Townsville, Queensland, an event which gave newspaper editors more than adequate copy, for Ellen Thompson's hysterical outbursts were virtually non-stop. Her claims of victimisation were interspersed with foul insults directed at witnesses, and on the final day of the trial she harangued the judge for three quarters of an hour on the subject of her own innocence and her devotion to her 'suicidal' husband. But it was to no avail; both were found guilty and, after being sentenced to death, were later put on board a steamer bound for Brisbane and its scaffold.

On the fateful day, 13 June 1887, both were led out to face the vast crowds who eagerly awaited the condemned woman's latest outburst, but during her incarceration, Ellen had evidently sought forgiveness in the Bible and now appeared on the scaffold holding a crucifix, her lips moving in prayer. But, her defiant spirit reasserting itself once more, she looked scornfully down on the spectators and shouted, 'Ah, soon I'll be in a land where people won't be able to tell lies about me! I will die like an angel!' Positioned on the drop, she stood still as Blackbeard, the executioner, drew the white cap down over her face and placed the noose around her neck. Stepping back, he pulled the lever; the trapdoors parted with a crash but the noise was instantly drowned by the screams and shouts from the onlookers as it became hideously obvious that the hangman had overestimated the length of rope needed. In falling too far, the noose had torn through the flesh, and now the victim's blood flowed copiously across the boards and into the pit! Nor was that all, for within minutes Harrison was similarly pinioned and noosed, his end coming in the same disastrous manner.

Before the official post-mortem took place, Professor Blumenthal, the phrenological expert, carefully measured the various curvatures and contours of the victims' skulls and then gave his considered analysis of their separate natures based on his findings. He declared that the woman showed every sign of being very combative and destructive, with extreme selfish and animal characteristics; her lover, John Harrison, although similarly combative, was incapable of being anything other than subservient to her.

Even without the learned professor's conclusions it was obvious that it was Ellen's greed and John's supine nature which led to their downfall – through the trapdoors.

In 1864 a gang attacked and murdered some American ranchers, five of the killers later being captured and sentenced to be hanged. They were escorted on to the scaffold and after they had been noosed, a spectator asked the executioner, 'Did you feel for the poor man when you put the rope around his neck?'

The hangman, one of whose friends had been killed by members of the gang, looked quizzically at his questioner. 'Yes,' he replied drily. 'I felt for his left ear.'

Jackie Whiston

An Aborigine, Jackie Whiston had committed a truly heinous crime, that of dragging 15-year-old Henrietta Reis into nearby bushes on 6 December 1869, and brutally assaulting her. He was subsequently arrested by the Toowoomba police and on 31 January 1870 was charged with rape. After a trial lasting only two hours, he was found guilty of that crime, one for which capital punishment was mandatory.

On 7 March 1870 the condemned man was escorted on to the makeshift scaffold which had been erected for the occasion. The weather was appalling, with heavy rain and strong winds which rocked the flimsy structure, and Jackie presented a miserable cowering spectacle as he mounted the steps. Blackbeard, the executioner, wet and impatient, quickly thrust his victim on to the drop and pinioned the man's arms and ankles.

Dropping the cap over Whiston's head, followed by the noose, he pulled the lever – only to see the man's feet somehow swing to one side, crashing into the crossbeam supports of the scaffold and become securely wedged there. The rope was taut, tightening the noose relentlessly about the man's throat, slowly strangling him. The crowd of spectators waited, listening in horror as at least four times during the next half hour they heard the sheriff ask whether life was finally extinct, then watched, aghast, as the two doctors present pressed their ears against the victim's chest – then shook their heads. Not until forty-five minutes passed was death eventually confirmed, the corpse then being cut down and buried in the Toowoomba Cemetery.

Falsely accused of treason by Titus Oates, William Howard, Viscount Stafford, mounted the scaffold on Tower Hill on 29 December 1680. He was loudly abused and jeered at by the rabble but when he appealed to the officials present, Sheriff Bethel, with brutal humour, replied, 'Sir, we have orders to stop nobody's breath but yours.'

Charles Thomas White

Why Charles White, a prosperous 23-year-old bookseller with an apparently thriving business in Holborn, London, would want to burn down his shop in order to defraud the insurance company was a complete mystery, but he did. And although the year of the Great Fire, 1660, was long gone, nevertheless in 1839 arson was still a capital offence, one which carried the death sentence.

After judgement had been passed on him and he was transferred to the condemned cell, his nerve broke; pacing up and down he constantly bewailed his fate and proclaimed his innocence. He made abortive attempts at escaping, all frustrated by his vigilant jailers. It was transparently obvious that on execution day, 2 January 1840, James Foxen, the hangman, and his assistant Thomas Cheshire, known with derisive affection to the scaffold crowd as Old Cheesy, were going to have a lot to contend with – and so it proved.

Pelham's Chronicles of Crime, published in 1886, made little effort to conceal the lurid details from the general public:

'he was escorted from his cell, and at length the procession moved on to the scaffold, where the wretched man mounted the platform at twenty minutes past eight, with a faltering and unsteady step. On the executioner and his assistant now approaching him in such a way as to convince him of their firmness, he became frightfully agitated, and he raised his arms and extended his chest, as if desirous of bursting the bonds which secured him. In the attempt he loosened the bandages around his wrists, and on the cap being drawn over his face, his terror seemed to increase. No sooner had Foxen left him, than he suddenly raised his arms and, by a violent motion, pushed off the cap; and accompanying this act with a motion of the body, he made a strong effort to liberate his neck from the halter.

Two assistant executioners were now called and, having approached the unhappy man, they held him while the cap was again placed over his face and tied there with a handkerchief. The miserable wretch during the whole of this time was struggling with the most determined violence, and the scene excited the strongest expressions of horror among the crowd. Upon his being left again, he advanced from the spot on which he had been placed, until he had got his feet nearly off the drop, and had rested them on the firm part of the platform; and almost at the same time he succeeded in tearing the handkerchief from his eyes.

The outraged feelings of the assembled populace were still to be excited by a more frightful exhibition than any they had yet witnessed; the accustomed signal having been given, the drop sunk; but the wretched man, instead of falling with it, suddenly jumped upon the platform and, seizing the rope around his throat with his hands, which he had sufficiently loosened by the violence of his struggles, he made an effort to prolong that life to which he seemed so strongly attached.

At this moment the spectacle was horrifying in the extreme. The convict was partly suspended, and partly resting on the platform. During his exertions his tongue had been forced from his mouth, and the convulsions of his body and the contortions of his face were truly appalling. The cries from the crowd were of a frightful description, and they continued until Foxen had forced the wretched man's hand from the rope, and, having roughly removed White's feet from the platform, had now caused all the man's weight to be sustained by the rope. The distortions of his countenance could even now be seen by the crowd, and as he remained suspended with his face uncovered, the spectacle was terrific. The hangman at length terminated his sufferings by hanging to his legs, and the unhappy wretch was seen to struggle no more.'

In 1793, on hearing that the practice of transporting felons from Newgate Prison to the Tyburn scaffold through City streets lined with crowds of eager onlookers would cease, the executions thereafter taking place outside the prison itself, the famous writer and lexicographer Dr Samuel Johnson exclaimed vehemently, 'The age is running mad after innovation! They object that the old method drew together a large number of spectators – Sir, executions are intended to draw spectators; if they do not draw spectators they don't answer their purpose. The old method was most satisfactory to all parties; the public was gratified by a procession; the criminal was supported by it. Why is all this to be swept away?'

John Young

The practice of including the time at which the condemned person should be hanged in Scottish death sentences led to misunderstandings, some victims assuming that their execution, if not completed by the specified time, would not be legal. One such misguided man, John Young of Edinburgh, a sergeant condemned to death in 1750 for passing forged banknotes, was sentenced to die between two and four o'clock, and so he made up his mind to delay matters until after that time when, he believed, he would be reprieved.

When, at two o'clock precisely, the magistrates and officials appeared at his cell door, he made the excuse that he wanted a few minutes alone with the minister. Somehow he persuaded the worthy clergyman to leave the cell for a moment, then he bolted the iron door and refused to open it again. Desperate attempts were made to force an entry and as the time passed towards four o'clock, the magistrates ordered all the clocks in the vicinity to be stopped! Meanwhile the onslaught on the cell continued, success finally being achieved when soldiers smashed their way in through the ceiling from the cell above. Young put up a frenzied resistance and after being knocked unconscious, was dragged headfirst down the stairs and carried out to the scaffold. There, he recovered consciousness and, it then being 4.15, he protested that they could not legally hang him, to which the executioner retorted that they could, even if it were nine o'clock at night! At that he continued his frantic struggles, proclaiming that 'he would not be an accessory to his own murder', his vehement objections continuing until the noose tightened relentlessly around his neck.

On 24 May 1725 Jonathan Wild, gangleader par excellence, was taken to Tyburn to be hanged. On the way, true to his principles, he picked the pocket of the chaplain accompanying him. Characteristic of the intemperate habits of Newgate Prison chaplains at that time, the item was a corkscrew, and Wild 'died with that eloquent trophy in his hand.'

Lethal Injection
James Autry

Even though many executions by this method have been carried out, it still is far from being fault-free. Execution by the firing squad, the rope, even the guillotine, is mainly dependent on the mechanical devices involved, i.e. the rifle, the trapdoor and the release of the blade, but in the lethal injection method difficulties arise in the insertion of tubes into the arm; the patient may not cooperate; there could be phlebitis if the patient has a history of taking drugs or if there have been previous attempts to insert the tubes. So even a method accepted as 'merciful' is not necessarily infallible.

In the 1980s, during the early days of lethal injection, teething troubles were bound to be encountered, and this was certainly the case during the execution of James Autry. Drunk, he had entered a store and picked up some cans of beer; on being asked to pay for them, he had produced a gun and shot the female assistant, killing her instantly. On fleeing from the shop he saw two men who might just have witnessed the murder, so he opened fire again, killing one and severely injuring the other. When captured and put on trial he denied all knowledge of the massacre, but the evidence, together with his criminal record, left the court no alternative but to sentence him to death by lethal injection.

On 5 October 1983, after a meal of hamburgers and chips, he was strapped on the trolley, the needles were inserted into his veins, and the first controlled flow, that of saline solution, commenced. Ten minutes or so later, as a result of a legal counter-argument, a stay of execution was granted, and just after midnight he was unstrapped and taken back to his cell. Callous murderer though he was, one cannot even begin to imagine his state of mind at the time, and the suspense of not knowing whether he was going to be executed or not continued for a further five months when, all appeals having been rejected, Autry found himself once again supine on the trolley. Once more the needles were inserted, the chemicals started to flow and the clock ticked away, dismay filling those who witnessed his slow death as fully ten minutes elapsed before the victim finally succumbed to the toxic cocktail.

Roger Gray was the Exeter hangman in the seventeenth century, when the noosed victim had to mount a ladder which was then turned, propelling him or her into eternity. A professional come what may, Roger did not hesitate when his own brother had to be hanged, afterwards writing to his nephew, 'I am sorry to be the conveyancer of such news unto you as cannot be very welcome. Your father died eight days since, but he was the most generous man I ever saw. I will say this of him everywhere; for I myself trussed him up. He mounted the ladder with good grace, but spying that one of the rungs was broken, and being a lover of good order, he turned to the sheriff and desired it might be mended for the next comer, who perhaps might be less active than himself.'

Peter Morin
Injection difficulties also occurred at Peter Morin's execution on 13 March 1985. A suspected serial killer, he was also a confirmed drug addict, the result being that, so scarred were his arms and legs, the technician spent forty minutes trying to insert the needles, but in vain – or vein. So although it was reported that the victim took only ten or so minutes to die after the final injection, in actual fact Morin's execution lasted fifty minutes; surely a barbaric and unacceptable way to dispatch a human being, no matter what his sins.

A victim of the French Revolution, Mme Jeanne Roland had very fine long black hair, and executioner Charles-Henri Sanson explained the need to crop her tresses short, lest they impeded the guillotine blade as it descended. Calmly she allowed him to wield his scissors, interrupting him only to say, 'At least leave me enough for you to hold my head up and show it to the people, if they wish to see it.'

The Sword
Marquis de Cinq-Mars

This French aristocrat, Henri Coiffier de Ruz, born in 1620, was the son of the Marshal d'Effiat and held the title of the Marquis de Cinq-Mars. Nor was this the only title he possessed, for by the age of nineteen he had been chosen to become equerry to King Louis XIII, his Majesty further favouring him by making him not only Grand Seneschal (steward) of France and Master of the Horse, but the most ostentatious of all, Monsieur le Grand, the King's confidant. Moreover he was granted the rare privilege of being present while the King discussed high affairs of state with his prime minister, Cardinal Richelieu, and was even permitted the liberty of putting his own suggestions forward. Such accolades and royal concessions, together with the power that went with them, went to the young man's head, magnifying his own importance to the stage where, by 1642, he began to have serious ambitions of actually replacing Richelieu as the King's personal adviser.

But the wily and experienced Cardinal had intelligence agents in every quarter of the royal court and he acted with ruthless speed; Cinq-Mars and his accomplice, the King's brother Gaston, Duke of Orléans, had barely started to discuss the means by which they could dispose of Richelieu, before both were arrested and put on trial, the court hearing to take place at Lyons.

What followed was almost unbelievable. The Cardinal, a sick man, was virtually bedridden, but was determined to attend the trial. Because of his condition, travel by carriage was out of the question, and so a portable wooden room was made for him. It was painted all over with gilt, and contained a bed, a table and a chair, while the walls were draped with crimson damask. It was transported on the heads of twenty of his bodyguards, and in much same way as lamp-posts, traffic lights and the like are removed in order to facilitate the passage of a wide load along major roads in this country, so for the Cardinal's caravan, walls, gateways, even houses, were demolished in order that its progress should not be obstructed or delayed. On reaching the river Rhône, it was transferred to a large barge which, together with another boat containing the two unfortunate prisoners, was then towed by horses to its destination.

The trial began at 7 a.m. and was all over in a matter of hours, the President of the court, Chancellor Sequier, being a personal enemy of Cinq-Mars, decreeing that not only should both traitors be beheaded by the sword, but that as the instigator, Cinq-Mars should be tortured before being taken to where the executioner awaited.

A Jesuit priest, Father Malavette, was appointed to minister to Cinq-Mars, the prisoner then exclaiming to him, '*Mon Pére*, they are going to torture me. I can scarcely bring myself to submit to it.' But the priest's reply hardly gave the doomed man any consolation. 'You must submit to the hand of God, Monsieur,' he said. 'Nothing ever happens except by his permission.'

The victim was then led to the torture chamber and although no details were divulged, it is likely that he suffered in the Boots, perhaps a version in which each leg was encased between boards in the manner of splints, both legs then being bound together. For the *question ordinaire*, that which persuaded the victim to admit his or her guilt, wedges would be driven between the two innermost boards with a mallet; for the *question extraordinaire*, requiring the divulging of the names of any fellow conspirators, four more wedges would be driven between the legs and the outer boards, crushing and eventually shattering the limbs.

Whatever methods were employed, it was reported that he had to be supported by warders on being led from the room.

Tightening The Screw-Type Boots

After a little wine and some bread, he prayed with his priest before writing to his mother, asking her to pay all his debts.

At 3 p.m. he and Gaston were taken by coach to the Place des Terrau, on the banks of the river Saône, where the scaffold had been erected. The thousands of spectators who packed the balconies and the area around the platform, even those perched precariously on the rooftops, greeted the traitors' arrival with cheers and cries of abuse. Supported by Father Malavette, Cinq-Mars mounted the scaffold steps with great difficulty but, with the bravado of youth, he then saluted the crowd. There was little doubt that he had dressed for the occasion, for he wore a court suit trimmed with gold lace, his black hat being ornamented with red feathers, his stockings were of green silk, and diamond buckles glittered on his fashionably high-heeled shoes. Over his arm he carried a large scarlet cloak, to be used to cover his body after his decapitation, and a contemporary chronicler reported that:

'his fair young face was perfectly serene, and his clustering curls, slightly powdered, were scented and tended as carefully as if he were in the royal presence. He bowed to the crowd, then replaced his hat on his head and looked about him. Nearby stood the executioner; he was only a city porter, the regular official being ill, and his replacement was a coarse and brutal fellow with a bloated face. When he approached Cinq-Mars with scissors to cut off his hair, Monsieur le Grand waved him away with a motion of disgust and instead begged Father Malavette to do him this office and to keep his hair for his mother.'

While the priest-turned-barber snipped away the long shoulder-length ringlets, Cinq-Mars turned to the executioner, who had not yet taken his sword out of the dirty bag which lay beside him and, according to the chronicle:

'asked him haughtily what he was about, and why he did not begin. The rude fellow making a wry face in reply, Cinq-Mars left him and said to the priest, '*Mon Pére*, assist me in my prayers, then I shall be ready.' After he had prayed very devoutly and kissed the crucifix, he rose from his knees and in a firm voice exclaimed, 'I am ready – begin.'

He threw aside his hat, unloosed the lace ruff about his throat and put back his hair from his face. But the executioner, being unready and new to his office, delivered no fewer than eleven blows ere his head was severed from his body. When it fell, it gave a little bound, turned itself a little to one side and the lips were seen to palpitate, the eyes being wide open. His body was then covered by the scarlet mantle and carried away to be buried.

Meanwhile, the King, having been previously informed by the Cardinal of the precise date and hour when Cinq-Mars would

THE EXECUTIONER ALWAYS CHOPS TWICE

suffer death, took out his watch at the precise time and, with the most perfect unconcern, remarked to a companion, 'At this moment Monsieur le Grand is making an ugly face at Lyons!'

A victim of political intrigue, in 1766 the Chevalier de la Barre refused to kneel for the French executioner Charles-Henri Sanson to behead him, saying, 'I cannot! I am no criminal – strike me as I am!' Whereupon Sanson, an expert with the heavy, two-handed sword, swung it so accurately that it severed the victim's spine and passed through the neck without dislodging the head from the shoulders. And true or false, as the victim's body started to sway, onlookers reported that they heard Sanson exclaim, 'Shake yourself – it is done!'

Thomas Arthur de Lally-Tollendal

One night in 1731 a group of young men left a bar in the suburbs of Paris after spending a convivial evening together and, losing their way entirely, found themselves on the Rue d'Enfer where they saw a house, the windows of which were brilliantly lit. They heard faint sounds of music and, peering through the gate, saw the figures of couples as they danced past the windows. The young men, somewhat elated by the wine they had been drinking, resolved to join in the fun; they boldly knocked on the door, requesting the servant who opened it, that they be allowed to participate in the revelry.

The master of the house appeared, a man of about 30, of distinguished appearance, the elegance of his dress suggesting that he was one of the upper classes. He greeted them with courtesy and listened to their request with the smile of a man who understood the foibles of youth. He informed them that the ball which was taking place was to celebrate his marriage, saying that he would be honoured if they would join the festivities, but adding that perhaps the company they wished to

216

join was not, perhaps, worthy of them. The young men, however, insisted, and the bridegroom, having conducted them to the ballroom, introduced them to his new wife and to his family.

On meeting the dancers the young men realised that, despite their pleasure, they all seemed to look very severe, an aspect which dampened the gaiety they had anticipated; their faces remained rather grim and sinister even while they expressed the goodwill they felt for the strangers. Some of the women, however, were pretty, and the young men, who were all of noble birth, were in high spirits, and too youthful and light-hearted to let that bother them, and they proceeded to dance the night away, thoroughly enjoying themselves.

At daybreak, the bridegroom, still smiling, told them that his name was Jean-Baptiste Sanson, that he was the Paris executioner, and that most of the gentlemen whose pleasures they had shared, followed the same profession.

Two of the young men were visibly disturbed by this piece of information, but the third one, who wore the uniform of Dillon's Irish Regiment, burst out laughing and said he had long wished to make the acquaintance of the official who decapitated, burned and broke (on the wheel) so many good people, and he was very glad now of having the opportunity. He then begged M. Sanson to have the kindness to show them his instruments.

Jean-Baptiste acceded to the request and led the party to a room used as the arsenal of his tools of torture and death. While the officer's companions were expressing their astonishment at the curious shapes of certain instruments, the young man examined the swords of justice with much attention. The executioner took one down and handed it to the officer, who looked at it carefully and, taking it with both hands, wielded it with uncommon strength and dexterity, meanwhile asking his host whether it was possible to strike off a head with it at a single

217

stroke. Jean-Baptiste answered in the affirmative, adding jokingly that if he, the officer, ever committed the same crimes as one Cinq-Mars, he, Jean-Baptiste, would pledge his word that he would not allow him to suffer! The young man thanked his host, little knowing that his curiosity might almost be termed a prediction of things to come, and then made his farewells, giving his name, Count Thomas Arthur de Lally-Tollendal.

Thirty-five years after that chance meeting, on 6 May 1766, the Parliament assembled in the Court of Justice and condemned the Commander of the French Forces in India, Lieutenant-General Thomas Arthur de Lally-Tollendal to death by the sword, for betraying the King.

De Lally-Tollendal was of Irish extraction and at the age of twelve obtained a commission in Dillon's Irish Regiment (of the French army), and later took part in the siege of Barcelona. By 1740 he commanded his own regiment and at the age of 37 he was promoted to Lieutenant General. Ambitious, possessing a strong streak of ruthlessness, he hated the English and even devised a plan involving the landing of 10,000 men on the English coast to support the Stuart Pretender, a scheme that was rejected by the French High Command who, however, gave him command of their colonial troops. But the unmitigated violence of his temper, his eschewal of any action other than brutal strength, led him to make appalling military errors. In India he captured Goudelour, swept along the Coromandel coast and took St David, where he permitted frightful excesses to be committed by his troops, who proceeded to ransack the town. Completely contemptuous of the Hindu religion, he allowed local revered sanctuaries to be violated, and caused any native suspected of spying to be blown from the mouth of a cannon. Against the advice of his generals, he later advanced northwards, only to be attacked by the English forces; in the retreat that followed, he lost a quarter of his troops and eventually had to surrender, together with most of his army, and was taken to England as a prisoner of war.

In France he was, probably correctly, made the scapegoat for the disastrous defeat, but on news of this slur on his honour reaching him, he was filled with outrage and obtained permission from the English Government to be released on parole in order to return to France and defend his reputation. But his enemies, of whom he had many, were only too pleased, and soon after his arrival, as a result of their machinations, he was imprisoned in the Bastille prison and put on trial, charged with treason, an ordeal which dragged on for nineteen months. Still full of an overwhelming sense of his own importance, his arrogance remained unabated.

On appearing before the judges he always wore the full uniform of a general, together with all the Orders which had been bestowed on him, but the President of the court ordered that he should be deprived of them. De Lally-Tollendal, protesting that he would rather be deprived of his life than the rewards of his bravery, resisted vehemently, but to no avail; in the struggle which followed, he fought with the soldiers as they tore his uniform and ripped off the epaulettes and decorations.

In court he was no more able to control his temper than when he had been in India. He disputed the evidence step by step, protesting against the charges, disputing, fuming, retorting, and accusing others of cowardice and the Government itself of failing to support him in the field. But there were too many witnesses testifying about his abuse of power, the cruelty to the natives, and the violence against all who dared to cross his path. And on 6 May 1766 the court found him guilty as charged.

After the sentence was read out, he remained dumbfounded and stupefied, but only momentarily, for he then started cursing, calling his judges assassins and executioners, and it was not until he had been taken back to the Bastille that he regained his composure. Some time later, however, he was approached by an intermediary who offered to raise a petition for his release; unfortunately the man mentioned the word 'crime' in connection with de Lally-Tollendal's military campaigns; at that, it was reported:

> 'the prisoner was overwhelmed by a fit of fury greater than any he had ever experienced before and, seizing a pair of compasses [a measuring instrument, both arms of which have sharp points] with which he had used to draw the map of the former scene of his successes and reverses, he stabbed himself near the heart. The weapon encountered a rib and only inflicted a slight wound; whereupon the gaolers rushed upon him and wrenched the instrument from his hand.'

The day of execution finally arrived, and, irony of ironies, his executioner was to be none other than Jean-Baptiste Sanson. He, recalling his promise made that night so many years ago, resolved to honour it to the full. Also on the scaffold would be his son, Charles-Henri, his assistance being essential, for Jean-Baptiste was now white-haired, and although only sixty, appeared to be much older, probably because of the stroke he had had some years earlier which had partially paralysed his right side. Accordingly, Jean-Baptiste selected from his collection the very sword which de Lally-Tollendal had handled while at the wedding party, and the two men went to the Bastille to collect their prisoner. There they found traces of a struggle which had just taken place, the authorities having decreed that in order to stop the victim inducing the crowds to attempt a rescue, he was to be gagged, and it was not until his fierce resistance had been overcome, that an iron gag was forced into his mouth.

Charles-Henri was about to order his assistants to escort the bound prisoner down the stairs when his father stepped forward, saying that he alone had a right to command. He knelt down before the Count and, perceiving that the cords were so tight that they almost cut into the flesh, ordered that they be slackened. De Lally-Tollendal looked down and, recognising him, smiled, a tear coming to his eye.

On reaching the scaffold he ascended the steps with firmness, then turned to the old executioner; at that, Jean-Baptiste, after showing him his withered arm, pointed to his son, who was standing at the other end of the scaffold in order to conceal the sword he was holding, and explained that he was too old to strike, and therefore his promise must be discharged by a stronger arm and a steadier hand than his. De Lally-Tollendal thanked him by an inclination of the head, whereupon Charles-Henri now approached, and was about to raise the sword when his father stopped him. With a firm hand he took the gag out of the Count's mouth and, bowing respectfully, said 'Monsieur le Comte, I am the master here. Just as it happened thirty-five years ago, so today you are my guest. Accept the supreme hospitality which I then promised you.'

De Lally-Tollendal then prayed, after which he asked Charles-Henri to untie his hands, but the younger Sanson explained that it was not allowed. 'Then,' said the victim 'help me take off this vest and give it to your father.' Charles-Henri obeyed, taking off the vest, which was made of gold Indian cloth, each button being a large ruby of the finest quality. The Count then exclaimed in a loud voice, 'And now, you can strike!' Charles-Henri raised the weapon and brought it down on the Count's neck, but the hair, which had not been cut but only drawn back, obstructed the blade; instead of decapitating the Count, it only inflicted a severe head wound.

According to the *Memoirs* of the Sansons:

> 'The blow was so violent that de Lally-Tollendal was struck down to the earth, but he sprang to his feet in an instant and glared at Jean-Baptiste with an expression of indignation and reproach. At the sight, the old executioner rushed towards his son and, suddenly recovering his former strength, he took the bloody sword from his son's hands and, before the cry of horror which rose from the crowd subsided, de Lally-Tollendal's head was rolling on the scaffold!'

A leader of the second Jacobite uprising, the 80-year-old Scot, Simon Fraser, Lord Lovat, climbed the steps to the scaffold on Tower Hill, London, in 1747, assisted by his two yeoman warders. Looking at the vast crowd assembled to watch his execution, he exclaimed, 'God save us! Why should there be such a commotion about taking off an old grey head that cannot manage to get up a few steps without three bodies to support it?'

George Praun

In seventeenth-century Germany, as indeed in England, beheading ranked as an honourable way of paying one's debt to society, hanging being reserved for thieves, robbers and other criminals of low birth. Master Franz Schmidt, public executioner for the city of Nuremberg from 1573 to 1617 recorded an execution that amazed him:

> 'George Praun, a cook and swordsman, stole 13 dollars from the bag of a youth from Greyffenberg who was travelling with him, putting stones in their place. After that he took 8 florins from him at Koppenhagen and a further 5 florins from him at Hamburg. At Vienna he stole a pair of white silk stockings from a man, and from a Walloon's wagon, a valise containing a blue

mantle and a pair of red hose, also a white satin doublet. I beheaded him with the sword, and when placed on the stone, his head turned several times as if it wanted to look about it; it opened its mouth and moved its tongue as if wanting to speak, for a good half quarter of an hour.'

The diary entry ended with his incredulous comment, 'I have never seen the like of it!'

Archibald Campbell, ninth Earl of Argyll, supported the abortive Monmouth Rebellion of 1685 and so was condemned to die on the Scottish Maiden, an early type of guillotine. The proud Earl, bowing his neck beneath its pendant blade, commented wryly that 'it was the sweetest maiden he'd ever kissed.'

Angelique Ticquet

She was young, she was rich, she was beautiful but, hating her elderly husband, she plotted to have him murdered.

Angelique Carlier, as she was then, was born in 1657, the daughter of an affluent printer and bookseller, and on his death she inherited a half-share in the large fortune he had bequeathed to her and her brother. Strikingly attractive, she never lacked male companionship in the social circles in which she moved, but wishing to move into the upper echelon of Paris society, she accepted the marriage proposal offered her by Pierre Ticquet, a well-to-do but elderly magistrate. He spared nothing in gratifying her every wish; on her birthday he presented her with a magnificent bouquet, the flowers being intermingled with diamonds and precious stones.

Their honeymoon lasted nearly three years, and they later took up residence in a splendid house in the city, where Mme Ticquet had her own carriage and horses, and daily entertained a host of guests in her drawing rooms. By constantly indulging

223

her, her husband, whose only income came from his office, frequently ran into debt, but she ignored all his protestations to economise with a petulance that slowly turned into an all-consuming hatred.

Among her guests was a certain captain in the French Guards Regiment, M. de Montgeorges, an elegant and handsome officer and, falling in love with him, an intimate relationship soon developed between them. Far from being discreet, she boasted about the affair to her friends, the news quickly reaching the ears of her husband, who wasted no time in putting a stop to her soirées and forbidding her gallant captain to enter the house. At that she vowed she would never lead the sort of domestic life her husband wanted to impose on her, and her aunt, agreeing with her, encouraged Pierre's many creditors to take legal proceedings against him. For her part, Angelique demanded a judicial separation from him, but her husband instantly responded by obtaining a *lettre de cachet* from the President of the Parliament, a blank order for imprisonment which simply required to be completed by the holder. Brandishing this in front of her, he demanded that she cancel her plans to separate, to be more submissive, and to dismiss the captain from her thoughts and her presence forever. Whereupon the outraged Angelique grabbed the document from him and threw it into the fire.

Unable to obtain another certificate, the cuckolded councillor became the laughing stock of Paris, this ridicule reinforcing Mme Ticquet's determination to rid herself of him one way or another and to marry the captain, whom she was still meeting. She therefore decided to have her husband killed, and she recruited her porter, Jacques Moura, as her accomplice, together with some of his friends. Later, though, she had second thoughts and cancelled the scheme. However Pierre Ticquet, doubting Moura's loyalty to him and suspecting that the porter was still admitting de Montgeorges to the building, dismissed the man and kept the keys to the house himself, thereby virtually imprisoning his wife. She, furious at the situation, then tried to poison him, sending her valet up to his room one night with a cup of broth, but the servant, suspecting her intentions and not wanting to become involved as an accomplice in a murder case, 'accidentally' dropped the cup and left the house. At that, by now frustrated beyond reason, Angelique decided that, come what may, her husband had to be killed.

A few nights later Tiquet had been visiting friends nearby and as he emerged from the house several shots rang out from the shadows and he fell, having been hit by five bullets, none of which, surprisingly, proved fatal. As the news spread, a criminal investigation was started and Moura, the porter, was immediately arrested, suspicion also falling on Angelique. Friends tried in vain to persuade her to flee; a monk actually offered to disguise her, probably as a nun, and escort her to Calais, where she could embark for England, but she refused to leave Paris and her captain. Within the next few days she was arrested.

Whatever defence she raised proved totally unsustainable when a man came forward and testified that he had been given money by Moura, on behalf of the accused, to take part in the first attempt to murder her husband, and as there was no evidence to substantiate charges regarding the third attempt, in which the shots were fired, she was tried and found guilty of conspiracy to kill.

In late May 1699 the sentence of the court 'condemned Angelique-Nicole Carlier to be decapitated in the Place de Gréve; Jacques Moura, her late porter, to be hanged; their property to be confiscated; and from her estate, ten thousand livres for the benefit of the King and one hundred thousand livres for her husband, to be extracted.' The compensation for M. Tiquet was subsequently increased to 120,000 livres by order of Parliament, but no appeal was allowed against the death sentence, despite the fact that the victim had survived the conspiracies.

It was essential that a full confession should be obtained, and also confirmation that all the would-be murderers had been rounded up, and the only way to achieve this was to torture the instigator of the plot. Accordingly Angelique was taken to the torture chamber, escorted by Criminal Lieutenant Deffita, paradoxically one of her earlier admirers. Upon refusing to divulge the information required, she was strapped to the bench, a cowhorn inserted into her mouth and, from a nearby tub, a jug was filled with water and poured into the funnel. Further refusals would have been countered by successive jugs of water, until eventually it would enter her lungs via her windpipe, causing death by drowning. However, Mme Ticquet, unable to face such an appalling fate, soon capitulated and confessed everything.

She was taken in the fatal cart, together with her spiritual adviser and Jacques Moura, the cortège slowly winding its way through the multitude of spectators, and finally reaching the site of execution. As usual she was clad in spotless white, her dress enhancing the beauty she still retained despite her 42 years. The vehicle had barely halted when a violent storm broke over the city, compelling the spectators to take cover in doorways and beneath balconies. On the scaffold two of the Sanson family – Monsieur de Paris having sent for his son – waited to do their duty. Delay was unavoidable, as it would have been suicidal to have attempted to swing the sword while standing on the wet, slippery boards, so executioners and victims had to sit for half an hour near the scaffold and next to the hearse which was there ready to transport Angelique's corpse to the cemetery.

At last the rain eased off. Jacques Moura was the first to be dispatched, then the older Sanson assisted the woman to mount the scaffold steps. As he did so, Angelique kissed his hand, grateful for the unspoken comfort he had given her. This touching gesture from such an elegant and composed woman about to be decapitated proved too much for Sanson; turning to his son he exclaimed, 'Take my place! My strength is failing me!'

Dutifully, if unwillingly, the young man stepped forward and waited until Mme Ticquet had prayed. She arranged her headdress, moving it clear of her slender neck and asked, 'Sir, will you be good enough to show me the position I am to take?' He answered, 'Kneel down with your head up, lift your hair away from your neck and let it fall forward over your face.' She obeyed, saying, 'Am I well thus?' He nodded, then stepped back and, gripping the heavy, two-handed sword, swung it round in an arc to gain momentum. As he did so, the woman, totally feminine to the very end, exclaimed, 'Be sure not to disfigure me!'

Sanson momentarily faltered at her interruption, his aim consequently going badly awry, the razor-sharp blade slashing across the side of her neck, the crowd gasping in horror at the sight of the blood as it poured from the gaping wound. Desperately Sanson struck again, the blade hissing through the air, but only inflicting yet another severe wound. Finally, as described in the Sanson family *Memoirs*, 'blinded by the blood which spurted at every stroke, Charles brandished the weapon a third time in a kind of frenzy. At last the head rolled at his feet. His assistants picked it up, and several witnesses asserted that even in death it retained its former look of calmness and beauty.'

Anne Boleyn, second wife of Henry VIII, was found guilty of infidelity and incest with her brother, and in 1536 was sentenced 'to be burnt within the Tower of London, or to have her head smitten off, as the King's

pleasure decrees.' It was decided that she should be beheaded with a sword, 'which thing had not before been seen in this land of England.' Sir William Kingston, the Constable of the Tower, wrote in his report, 'I told hyr it sholde be no payne, it was so sottle [subtle]; and then she sayd, I have hard say the executioner was very gud and I have a lyttel nek, and she put her hand about it, laffyng hartely.'

The Wheel
Louis Dominique Cartouche

To be broken on the wheel was assuredly one of most barbaric of all methods of execution, even for as notorious a criminal as Cartouche. Gangleader, highwayman and robber, he and his men preyed on French shops and banks, coaches, chateaux and ordinary pedestrians, the public breathing a deep sigh of relief when, on 15 October 1721, the police announced his capture. Despite being only four and a half feet tall, thin, with a large head and thinning hair, according to the Paris executioner Charles Sanson, the felon possessed an almost hypnotic power over women. 'It was,' the hangman said, 'surprising that a man so ugly should be represented as a lady-killer.'

The authorities had been trying to capture him for years, but eventually his gang was infiltrated by a spy, Duchatelat, who eventually reported that the wanted man could be found at a wine dealer's house in La Courtelle. Forty fully armed soldiers led by the Secretary of State for War, M. le Blanc, attacked his hide-out. There they found him in bed and managed to overpower him before he had a chance to seize one of the six loaded pistols lying on his bedside table. Arrested, he was taken to Chatelet Prison, there to be chained to a stone pillar, with four men guarding the cell's triple doors. But Cartouche refused to be defeated; he and his cell-mate, an ex-mason, dug down into the earthen floor, breaking into a sewer. Wading through the effluent, they hacked their way through a side wall, to discover that they then stood in a greengrocer's cellar. The owner, alerted to their presence by the barking of his dog, was sympathetic towards the escapers and led them out to the street, but unfortunately a passing police patrol saw them and, possibly realising by the chains still attached to their wrists and ankles that they were not customers doing a little late shopping, captured the pair and took them to the Conciergerie, the main prison.

Put on trial on 26 November 1721, Cartouche displayed his usual happy-go-lucky attitude in the court, but his nonchalant air faded as the sentence was read out; he and five members of his gang were first to endure the *question ordinaire et extraordinaire*, i.e. to be interrogated while receiving the lesser and greater tortures of the torture chamber, then to be broken on the wheel. Then, as much information as possible having been extracted from him by the application of the torture of the Boots and other fiendish devices, the crippled felon was taken in the cart to the Place de Gréve, where the scaffold, surrounded by an immense crowd, had been erected.

It was a truly spectacular occasion, one long awaited by the populace, and the square was packed, a contemporary journal describing how, 'All night long, carriages transported passengers to the Place until it was jammed with people. Windows facing the square were lit all night. The cold was biting, but the people lit fires right in the square and the local merchants sold food and drink. Everyone was laughing, drinking, singing, and celebrating. Most of the spectators had had their places reserved for over a month.'

En route to the scaffold Cartouche started to show signs of agitation and when he saw the fearsome cartwheel mounted on its upright axle, he turned pale, beads of perspiration forming on his brow. All cynicism now long gone, nevertheless on being secured to the Croix de St André, the St Andrew's Cross, of planks nailed to the face of the wheel, he managed to call out 'One!' when Sanson delivered the first blow with the iron bar, fracturing part of one limb, but then lapsed into silence.

No matter how serious the crimes committed by a criminal, the court usually gave him the benefit of the retentum, a fatal blow to the heart after a certain number of strokes, and that merciful clause had been included in Cartouche's sentence, but due to an appalling error by a clerk, Sanson was not informed, and so the sickening procedure had to be meted out in full. More blows rhythmically rained down on the victim, shattering his arms above and below his elbows, and his legs above and below his knees. Cartouche eventually received eleven blows with the bar, and it was reported that he was still alive twenty minutes after first being strapped to the wheel.

Broken On The Wheel

The persuasive capability of the instruments in the torture chamber was such that an almost complete round-up of the remaining members of the Cartouche gang then swung into action. More than 150 of them were arrested, many subsequently being hanged; renegade jewellers, informers, receivers and collaborators were also caught and suitably punished. Nor were those women and children associated with the mob spared; Cartouche's animal magnetism where women were concerned was never more evident than when five of his mistresses were taken into custody and later hanged on Sanson's scaffold, and the gangleader's brother, although only fifteen years of age, was sentenced not only to hard labour for life, but was also the first to suffer an unusual and unnatural punishment, the brain-child of Judge Arnould de Boueix.

In revenge for the recent murder on the highway of his father, a police officer, he ordered that the boy 'be suspended under the armpits for two hours in the Place de Grève.' Accordingly, Sanson and his assistants obeyed, placing the noose around his chest, but the boy's frantic screams and protestations that he would rather die than endure such pain, faced them with a predicament, one that was only solved by the executioner deliberately disregarding the judge's instructions; on seeing the lad's face being suffused with blood and then being unable even to whisper, he cut down their victim long before the specified two hours had elapsed and ordered that he be returned to the prison. Regrettably however, the boy died without regaining consciousness.

When, in 1535, Sir Thomas More was ordered to position his head on the block, 'he, having a great grey beard, said to the Executioner, "I pray you let me lay my Beard forward over the Block lest you should cut it off; for though you have a Warrant to cut off my Head, you have none to cut off my Beard!"'

A Happy Ending?

Although, in most of the countries referred to in this book, many of the methods of execution are still being administered and the scope for their associated gaffes therefore continues unabated, one method at least will never bring untold agony to its victims ever again, the abolition of being 'broken on the wheel' allowing this book at least to finish with a Happy Ending.

The event which brought this about started with a domestic quarrel over politics. In 1788 an elderly, conservative-minded blacksmith, Mathurin Louschart, and his family lived in a house in the Rue de Satory in Versailles. Mathurin, much respected by the local community, had a son, Jean, whom he loved dearly, even when the young man, instead of wanting to follow in his father's footsteps around the anvil, started to show signs of having radical ideals.

One day at dinner, as related in the Sanson *Memoirs*:

'Jean, carried away by his enthusiasm, extolled the socialist merits of Voltaire and Rousseau; Master Louschart was at first astounded at his audacity, but his stupefaction was soon replaced by anger. A dispute followed and Jean was peremptorily ordered to hold his tongue. The young man, although respectful, was passionate and headstrong, and disobeyed the injunction, retorting that his father had a novel way of settling a discussion. This did not mend matters, and at length his father showed him the door. It was in vain that Jean expressed his regret and readiness to apologise; the old smith would listen to no excuse, and turned him out.'

Now it so happened that a Mme Verdier, a distant relative, was also living in the house, and she had a very attractive daughter, Helen. Helen and Jean thought a lot of each other, which is more than could be said of Helen's mother who, on hearing of the controversy, encouraged Mathurin to have nothing further to do with his son; moreover her influence over him was so great that she actually urged him to become Jean's rival and seek to marry Helen, at the same time ordering her daughter to forget all about Jean and prepare to accept Mathurin's proposal of marriage.

Helen could never accept this, and she and Jean made secret plans to elope. Accordingly, Jean kept the rendezvous outside his father's house but, instead of being joined by his sweetheart, he heard her screams from inside; breaking the door down, he rushed in to discover that her mother had found out their intentions and was now thrashing her unmercifully while his father looked on.

The *Memoirs* continued:

'Jean sprang forward to protect Helen, but his father stopped him and, with the utmost violence, upbraided him for what he styled his infamous conduct. Mme Verdier now came forward and goaded the old smith to such a climax of fury that he spat in his son's face. Jean had suffered in silence up to now, but this last insult was too much for his temper and he retorted with words of extreme bitterness. At this, Mathurin's rage knew no bounds; he seized a crowbar and aimed a terrific blow at his son.

The passage in which this scene took place was so narrow that the bar struck against the wall as it came down, and Jean was able to leap aside. Helen, who was watching with terror, cried to Jean to fly. The young man followed her advice and made for the door while his father was raising the crowbar for the second time, but the woman Verdier had anticipated Jean's intention and was resolutely standing against the door. Mathurin struck a second blow, and again missed his aim. As he was raising it for the third time, Jean rushed past him and tried to enter the workshop, whence he intended to jump through the window into the street, but the door to the workshop was locked and his father was giving chase; as he tried to break it open, a heavy piece of iron whizzed just above his head and struck one of the panels, which it shattered to pieces. Old Louschart had laid down his crowbar and had hurled his heavy hammer. He now came up and grappled with Jean, who now felt that the only way he could save his life was to master him; disarming his father, he tore himself away from the older man's grasp and took to his heels. As he was crossing the threshold, hardly knowing what he was about, he threw the hammer behind him and rushed out. So rapid was his flight that he did not hear a cry from the workshop – Master Mathurin had just risen from the ground; the heavy mass of iron, the hammer, had struck him above the right eye and, fracturing his skull, had killed him instantly.'

The consequences were as expected; the crime of patricide was so rare that from the meanest cottage to the royal court it was the only topic of conversation, and the King himself ordered the Public Prosecutor to proceed against the culprit without a moment's delay. Mme Verdier's evidence, that she had witnessed Jean deliver the fatal blow, was sufficient proof, but when Jean was arrested, he was shocked and dismayed, for he had been totally unaware that the hammer had even struck his father; so shocked in fact that when taken back to the house, he rushed forward to his father's corpse and passionately kissed the pale face, a gesture which was immediately dismissed as one of sheer hypocrisy by the local magistrate.

The public at first condemned Jean as a brutal murderer, but their sentiments slowly started to swing in his favour, not least when they realised that it must indeed have been a terrible accident and that he had been the victim of the acrimonious temper and vicious nature of Mme Verdier. So strong was their support that although at his trial the court found him guilty and sentenced him to death, they did not insist on the usual *amende honorable*, a punishment which included the prior amputation of the hand that had struck the blow, and by way of further mitigation, they stipulated that although he was to be broken on the wheel, he was to be secretly strangled before all his limbs were shattered.

But public opinion had already come to the conclusion that Jean was innocent of murder, and the news that his forthcoming execution would take place on 3 August caused wild excitement. Henri Sanson wrote:

'On the morning of the previous day my grandfather [Charles Henri Sanson] sent from Paris two carts containing the instruments of torture, and beams and boards for the erection of the scaffold. He himself went to Versailles in the afternoon. News of the rising emotions of that city's residents had not reached the capital and Charles Henri was so thoroughly convinced that he had to deal with a common criminal that he was greatly surprised when he found the whole town in a fever. The Place Saint-Louis was covered with so great a multitude that his assistants and carpenters could hardly go on with their work. No hostility was manifested, however; the crowd was noisy but its mood was gay; the name of Jean was scarcely mentioned, and the workmen who were erecting the scaffold were merely jeered. However, when one of the carpenters struck an urchin who was throwing stones at him, cries of 'Death!' were uttered; in an instant all the mocking faces became dark and threatening. The assistants and carpenters were attacked and their lives were in great danger. But a body of about a hundred men, easily identified as smiths by their athletic proportions and brawny faces, interfered, and partly by strength, partly by persuasion, they induced the crowd to retreat.

So far, my grandfather had not bestowed much attention to this popular demonstration, but he became more attentive when the interference of the smiths took place. He directed his assistants to finish the erection of the scaffold as quickly as possible, then he returned to Paris and lost no time in acquainting the authorities with his apprehensions.

The multitude which had thronged the Place Saint-Louis retired during the night; only a few young men remained to watch what took place around the scaffold. Meanwhile Charles Henri took what precautions he could, causing a strong paling [fence] to be erected around the scaffold, and on their side, the magistrates took it upon themselves to advance the hour of execution.

It was two o'clock in the morning when my grandfather went to the prison, to find Jean Louschart stretched out on his pallet when he entered the condemned cell. The doomed man rose and calmly surveyed him. The clerk of the Parliament read aloud the sentence, to which he listened with much attention. He then murmured a few words, among which only those of 'Poor father!' were heard, and he added in a loud voice, 'In two hours I shall justify myself before him!' Then, on being told that it was time to depart for the scaffold, he turned to the executioner, saying, 'You can be in no greater hurry than I am, sir.'

At half past four the cart moved in the direction of the Place Saint-Louis. The executive magistrates were in hopes that because of the granting of merciful retentum, the whole affair could be quickly over and done with before the population awoke, but they soon perceived their mistake, for the streets were swarming with people, the whole population was astir. Deafening clamours broke from the crowd as the cart appeared, and it was with the greatest difficulty that it made its way. The prisoner did not even seem to suspect that all this tumult was caused by the sympathy people felt for him. At the corner of the Rue de Satory a piercing cry was heard and a girl was seen waving her handkerchief. Jean Louschart looked up and, rising to his feet, he tried to smile, and exclaimed, 'Farewell, Helen, farewell!' At that moment a smith of tall stature and Herculean proportions who was walking near the cart, cried in a thundering voice, 'It is *au revoir* you should say, Jean. Are good fellows like you to be broken on the wheel?'

One of the guards on horseback drove him away, but applause

and cheers came from every quarter. It was obvious by the pale faces of the Parliament clerk, the policemen and the soldiers surrounding the cart that the agents of the law were anything but confident. The scaffold, however, was reached without accident. The crowd was thickly packed in the Place Saint-Louis, and as the cart stopped, Jean Louschart addressed a question to the priest who was sitting near him, and my grandfather heard the latter reply, 'To save you.' The doomed man said in a feverish voice and with some impatience, 'No, father, even if I am innocent of the intention of committing the crime, my hands are nevertheless stained with blood. I must die, and I wish to die – be quick, sir,' he added to my grandfather.

'Sir,' exclaimed Charles Henri, pointing to the infuriated masses who were already breaking through the palisade, 'if there is a man in danger of death here, it is not you!'

Hardly were the words out of his mouth than a tempest of groans and screams burst forth. The paling was broken and trodden underfoot, and hundreds of men rushed on to the scaffold. The smith who had earlier spoken to Jean was among the foremost; he seized the prisoner in his muscular arms, cut his bonds, and prepared to carry him off in triumph. An extraordinary scene now took place; Jean Louschart struggled violently against his saviours, then turned to the executioner and begged for death with the earnestness usually displayed by other culprits in asking for mercy. But his friends surrounded him and at length succeeded in carrying him away.

My grandfather's position was now perilous in the extreme; separated from his assistants, alone amidst a crowd that knew him only too well, he really thought that his last hour was at hand. His countenance probably betrayed his apprehensions, for the tall smith came up to him and seized his arm; 'Fear nothing, Charlot,' the smith exclaimed [Charlot was his nickname, which was also bestowed on subsequent executioners, in the same way as English hangmen were all called 'Jack Ketch' after an earlier executioner]. 'We don't want to harm you, but your equipment;

henceforth Charlot, you must kill your customers without making them suffer first.' And turning to the crowd he added, 'Let him pass, and take care he is not hurt.'

This harangue calmed the crowd, and my grandfather was allowed to withdraw. In less time than it takes to write this account, the scaffold and all its accessories were broken into pieces, which were then thrown on to the pile of wood prepared for the burning of the victim's mutilated body, and the terrible Wheel was placed on the summit as a kind of crown. The heap was set ablaze, and men and women, holding each other by the hand, formed an immense ring and danced around the crackling pile until it was reduced to ashes.'

Upon news of the debacle reaching the ears of King Louis XVI in Paris, he granted a pardon to Jean Louschart; nor was that all, for he decreed that the penalty of being broken on the wheel should be abolished with immediate effect. Regrettably history does not record whether Jean married his Helen – one would certainly like to think so.

SELECT BIBLIOGRAPHY

Abbott, G. *Rack, Rope & Red-Hot Pincers* (Dobby, 2001)
Abbott, G. *The Book of Execution* (Headline, 1994)
Abbott, G. *Family of Death* (Hale, 1995)
Andrews, W. *Old Time Punishments* (Andrews, 1890)
Andrews, W. *England in Days of Old* (Andrews, 1897)
Anonymous *The Record of Crimes, Judgements, Providences & Calamities* (1825)
Barington, S. *Errors and Executioners* (David & Layton, 1909)
Berry, J. *My Experiences as an Executioner* (Percy Lund)
Bleakley, H. *Hangmen of England* (Chapman & Hall, 1929)
Bryan, G. *Off with His Head!* (Hutchinson, 1934)
Calcraft, W. *The Life & Recollections of William Calcraft* (1870)
Carment, J. *Glimpses of the Olden Times* (Jackson, 1893)
Croker, J. W. *History of the Guillotine* (Murray, 1853)
Davey, R. *The Tower of London* (Methuen, 1914)
Elliot, R. H. *Experiences of a Planter in the Jungles of Mysore* (Chapman & Hall, 1871)
Elliot, R. G. *Agent of Death: The Memoirs of an Executioner* (John Long, 1941)
Evelyn, J. *Evelyn's Diary* (Bickers Bush, 1879)
Fox, C. *General Williamson's Diary* (Camden Society, 1912)
Gordon, C. *The Old Bailey & Newgate* (Fisher Unwin, 1902)
Holinshed, R. *Chronicles* (1586)
Jackson, W. *The New & Complete Newgate Calendar* (London, 1818)
Lacroix, P. *Manners, Customs & Dress in the Middle Ages* (1874)
Lawes, L. E. *Twenty Thousand Years in Sing Sing* (Constable, 1932)
Lenotre, G. *The Guillotine & Its Servants* (Hutchinson, 1929)
Machyn, H. *Diary of a London Resident* (Camden Society, 1848)
Marks, A. *Tyburn Tree* (Brown & Langham, 1908)
Sanson, H. *Memoirs of the Sansons* (Chatto & Windus, 1876)
Schmidt, F. *A Hangman's Diary* (Philip Allan, 1928)
Stow, J. *A Survey of London* (1720)
Swain, J. *Pleasures of the Torture Chamber* (Douglas, 1931)
Timbs, J. *Curiosities of London* (David Bogue, 1855)
Verdene, G. *La Torture* (R. Dorn, 1906)
Younghusband, Sir G. *The Tower of London from Within* (Jenkins, 1918)
Saturday Magazine series, 1833
Tyburn Gallows, London County Council, 1909
Calendar of State Papers, Domestic Series
Tower of London Records